CROSS WAYS®

1 SECTION

UNITS 1-10
From Creation to the Transjordan

Fourth Edition

Harry Wendt

CROSSWAYS INTERNATIONAL
Minneapolis, MN

CROSSWAYS®— SECTION 1
was developed and written by
Harry Wendt, Minneapolis, MN

Illustrations by
Knarelle Beard, Adelaide, South Australia

The Bible text in this publication is from the New Revised Standard Version of the Bible, copyright 1989 by the Division of Christian Education of the National Council of Churches of Christ in the United States of America and used by permission.

CROSSWAYS®— SECTION 1
is published and distributed by
CROSSWAYS INTERNATIONAL
7930 Computer Avenue South
Minneapolis, MN 55435
www.crossways.org

ISBN 1-891245-18-X

Fourth Edition

10 9 8 7 6 5 4 3 2

A Welcome from Crossways International!

We at Crossways International (CI) are delighted that you are about to undertake a study of the entire sweep of the Old and New Testaments using our materials as your guide. May your journey be fruitful and rewarding, and draw you ever closer to the mind, manner, and meaning of Jesus, the Servant-Messiah.

CI is more than a publisher of Christian education and Bible study materials. We also offer hands-on training in the use of our materials, and we make our materials available to special ministries and missions all around the world. We would be happy to partner with you in *any way* that might help you to share the Good News of God's Kingdom with the people you reach.

The courses of Crossways International have been translated into dozens of languages and are used by all major Christian denominations in numerous countries around the world. We have trained tens of thousands of pastors, teachers, and lay-people to teach the Bible with joy and passion.

WHAT DISTINGUISHES CROSSWAYS INTERNATIONAL?

1 A Panoramic View of Scripture

CI's courses examine the meaning of the Bible by digging into the *complete story* that runs through it—from *Genesis to Revelation*. We believe you cannot fully grasp the enormity and profundity of Jesus the Messiah's mind and message without understanding what preceded Him and set the stage for His ministry and mission.

2 Visual Learning

All of CI's teaching materials make extensive use of specially designed *color graphics* to help people better understand and remember the written material. These make it easier to share God's Good News.

3 Focus on Jesus, the Servant-King

We are not about biblical study merely for study's sake. The core of every CI course is *Jesus, the King who washed feet*—the Messiah who invites us to follow Him by loving and serving others—as He did. These courses help to *transform hearts and lives*.

4 Tools for Faith Development

CI offers *survey courses of increasing depth* that lead people through the entire story of the Bible—plus *short courses* on specific biblical topics, such as Jesus' parables, Christian stewardship, prayer, the Passion and the Christmas stories.

5 Workshop Training for Teachers & Laity

For those interested in *revitalizing their ministries* using CI's courses, we offer workshops that train attendees, step-by-step, how to do it. We also offer workshops for lay-people who are eager to boost their biblical literacy and steep themselves in Scripture. Call us or visit our website.

6 Mission Around the World—and at Home

CI's dedication to the mission and message of Jesus goes beyond mere publishing and teacher-training. We make our materials available in the U.S. and all around the world in *prisons, hospitals, orphanages, street ministries*—anywhere the need is great but resources are scarce. CI is a *non-profit ministry* that relies on our modest sales and the benevolence of supporters in our efforts to heed the Great Commission to "go and make disciples of all nations."

Contact Crossways International at 1-800-257-7308 or visit our website at <u>www.crossways.org</u>.

Acknowledgements

First Edition, 1979

Crossways does not pretend to be an original work. It reflects insights gleaned over the years from many sources, including instructors at Concordia Seminary, Adelaide, South Australia, 1951–55; instructors in the graduate school of Concordia Seminary, St. Louis, MO, U.S.A., 1967–71; and numerous books and commentaries.

I am deeply indebted to Australian graphic artist, Knarelle Beard, for her contribution to the production of this volume. The quality of her work, and manner in which she goes about it, reflect Christian discipleship at its best.

I am grateful also to a number of friends in Adelaide, South Australia, whose encouragement and help during the early stages of producing *Crossways* were valuable. I am particularly grateful to several members of the faculty of Luther Seminary, North Adelaide, for their help in reviewing the manuscript. A warm word of thanks must also go to the members of my family. They put up with talk of *Crossways* for several years, and helped in meaningful ways with the production of the manual. Now that the task is done, we commit the use of *Crossways* into the hands of our gracious Lord.

Second Edition, 1984

The first *Crossways* seminar in the United States was offered in Indianapolis, Indiana, June 4–8, 1979. To date, approximately 125 seminars have been offered in the United States, Canada, and Australia. Now, some five years later, a second edition of *Crossways* is being offered. The text has been rewritten and simplified, and new insights included. Many more illustrations have been added. Most of these were done by the original illustrator, Knarelle Beard. Some were done by Jay Mackay, Perryville, MO. We offer this second edition to the people of God with the prayer that it will lead them on a meaningful journey through the Holy Scriptures.

Third Edition, 1994

It is now 15 years since the first *Crossways* seminar was offered. Since that time, hundreds of seminars have been conducted in about 25 countries to introduce *Crossways* and spin-off courses such as *See Through the Scriptures* and *The Divine Drama*—and the list continues to grow. The text in the third edition of Crossways has been rewritten and restructured, and many of the graphics have been improved. The materials have been produced in a form that will make them easier to teach and study, and adapt for international use. I continue to thank God for the help of my illustrator, Knarelle Beard. Her work is making it possible to teach the Word not only to the well-educated, but also to many others in a world in which hundreds of millions of people are functionally illiterate.

Fourth Edition, 2006

Twelve years since the third edition and 27 years since the first! New insights have been added, and every effort has been made to make the layout of the written text more "user friendly." The illustrations have been upgraded, a number of new ones have been added, and all are now printed in full-color.

I am grateful to members of Crossways International's staff who read and re-read the written text, and made hundreds of helpful suggestions. Those persons are Dee Ryan, Evan Hansen, and Timothy Schaefer.

Australian graphic artist Knarelle Beard began working with me in 1978. The contribution she has made to the ministry of Crossways International is enormous. Her illustrations have made it possible to share the message of God's Good News with millions of people around the world.

In all things, to God be the glory!

Harry Wendt
August 2006

Foreword

Students who wish to enroll at Al-Azhar University in Cairo to study Islam must prior to admission have memorized the Qur'an. In Malaysia, government employees who memorize the Qur'an receive a salary increase. The Qur'an is the same length as the New Testament.

In the western world few Christians feel little desire to memorize even a single book of the New Testament. Biblical illiteracy is on the increase. Unless this is corrected, church membership will continue to decline. After all, if we no longer take our stand on the Bible, on what do we take it?

There are numerous reasons why the Bible has become an unfamiliar book to many people. One must feel a certain sympathy with those well-intentioned people who set out to read through the Bible, only to give up about halfway through Leviticus. They give up because they find it perplexing and incomprehensible, and have difficulty relating its message to life in today's world. The result is that many content themselves with an ability, acquired in childhood, to quote a few favorite passages, and comfort themselves with the thought that such passages contain all the truth they need to know to be saved. The result is that a growing number of people are content with a limited use of the Book they profess to be the Word of God.

A partial use of the Bible can be a dangerous thing. It is not good enough to confine one's interest in the Bible to snippets from the Psalms, and bits and pieces from the Prophets, the Gospels, and the Letters. To do this is to run the risk of missing the real message of these "favorite texts," which can be found only by studying them in their larger context.

Furthermore, to separate the Old and New Testaments into watertight compartments can lead to a misuse of Scripture. Only when we have come to grips with the story-line that runs through the Old Testament can we hope to understand the message of the New Testament fully.

It is significant to remember that the Bible our Lord used was the Old Testament. If we wish to understand what Jesus continues to say to us today, we must understand the story-line of the Old Testament, and how Jesus interpreted that story-line in relation to His person and ministry.

Crossways is not a course that will give lay-persons quick passage into the ordained ministry of the church. Nonetheless, it will provide serious students with a survey of the biblical narrative and the themes that surface within it—and their implications for all who live on Planet Earth.

Harry Wendt

God Rescues His People

These two illustrations are used throughout the Crossways series to depict the two key events of the biblical narrative.

The one on the left represents the Exodus from Egypt, the Covenant at Sinai, the Wilderness Wanderings, and, finally, entry into the Promised Land.

The one on the right represents an Exodus or "rescue event" of another sort—God's rescue of His people, not from a foreign oppressor, but from sin, death, and the powers of the demonic realm. This second— and infinitely profound—rescue event came in the form of Jesus' life as a servant-without-limit, His sacrificial death on a cross, His resurrection, and His eternal presence among us following the Ascension.

The first rescue event, or Exodus, is the cornerstone of the Old Testament; the second Exodus is the cornerstone of the New Testament.

The Logo of the *Crossways* Series

Crossways is a survey course of the biblical narrative and its major themes. The name is a composite of two words, *cross* and *ways*. In the course logo, the name is attached to a circle containing an empty cross, beneath which stand two persons with their arms raised in praise.

At the center of the circle stands the cross, the pivotal point of God's dealings with humanity. The cross is empty. The One who died on it is risen, alive, and present among us as the living Lord of heaven and earth, time and eternity.

In the circle are two people. There is no such thing as private Christianity. Jesus calls us to personal faith, but never to private faith. Either the Christianity destroys the privacy, or the privacy destroys the Christianity. The Christian walk is always done in community. God redeems us from bondage to self to live in a joyous, caring relationship with God and others.

People who come face to face with the cross stand at a Crossways in life. The cross summons them to decide whether they want Jesus the Messiah, who was once nailed to it, to be not only their Savior from sin but also their Lord in life. If they wish to have Jesus as their Lord, they must let Him teach and empower them to walk the way of the cross. To walk the way of the cross is to walk the way of a servant of God and others, full-time.

Around the cross and the people is a circle. People who want to get the most out of a 360-degree movie-in-the-round must take their stand in the center of the theater and look all around. The goal of *Crossways* is to equip the serious Bible student to stand in the center of the divine revelation, and take in the full sweep of God's redemptive plan.

The Anglican Catechism, in the section titled *The Church*, asks three key questions, and offers a pointed answer to each:

1 **Question:** What is the mission of the Church?

Answer: *The mission of the Church is to restore all people to unity with God and each other in Christ.*

2 **Question:** How does the Church pursue its mission?

Answer: *The Church pursues its mission as it prays and worships, proclaims the Gospel, and promotes justice, peace, and love.*

3 **Question:** Through whom does the Church carry out its mission?

Answer: *The Church carries out its mission through the ministry of all its members.*

May *Crossways* equip many to help God's people achieve their God-given mission.

Using *Crossways*

Good teaching is not lecturing; it is the art of assisting discovery. An old adage says:

Tell me, and I will forget.
Show me, and I will remember.
Involve me, and I will understand.

Those who study *Crossways* will on occasion be *told* and *shown* some things. However, the materials are structured to get people *involved* in a "hands-on" study of the biblical text, and discussion concerning its meaning and application for life.

The written text is supported by an extensive body of graphics. The illustrations are designed to equip group leaders to take seriously the old Chinese saying, "A picture is worth a thousand words." In the fourth edition of *Crossways*, the written text and study questions are tied much more closely to the teaching graphics.

Crossways is not meant to replace the Bible. It is designed to serve as a road map to help people make an exciting and meaningful journey through the "big story" that unfolds within the written Scriptures.

There is no substitute for reading the Bible itself. Those who wish to understand its message need to have more than a nodding acquaintance with its contents. The Bible yields its treasures to those who immerse themselves in its narrative and themes.

Crossways is designed for use with adults. Jesus taught adults and played with children. Unfortunately, in many parts of the Christian church today, the opposite is being done. The hope is that adults who study *Crossways* will feel moved, perhaps compelled, to teach children God's truth in a meaningful way.

People who believe that the Bible is a book intended for children are usually content to leave it behind when they themselves leave childhood behind. Those who begin to discover the Bible's central message will continue to saturate themselves in it and, if they are parents, will seek to plant in the minds and hearts of their children spiritual seeds that will blossom into a lifelong relationship with Jesus the Messiah.

Although *Crossways* is divided into six sections of ten units each that can be purchased separately, the hope is that people will work through all 60 units in chronological order. If people are to understand Jesus, they need to understand the story-line that leads up to Jesus. If they do not understand the "big picture" of the biblical narrative, they run the risk of de-historicizing Jesus and lifting Him out of the context of Judaism. When this happens, much of the profundity and enormity of Jesus' ministry and message is obscured.

The Bible yields countless treasures to those who dig into its contents persistently and deeply. May the use of *Crossways* help you unearth many precious spiritual gems.

The Structure of the *Crossways* Series

Crossways is offered in six sections of ten units each. Although each section is available for separate purchase, would-be students of the Bible are encouraged to work through all six sections in sequence to gain an overview of the Bible's "big picture." If they choose not to do that, they should first work through a course that will give them an overview of the biblical story-line, such as Crossways International's *See Through the Scriptures* or *The Divine Drama—The Biblical Narrative*. The six sections of *Crossways* are:

SECTION 1 — From Creation to the Transjordan

Creation; the biblical overture; the patriarchal narratives; the Exodus from Egypt; the Sinai covenant and the Pentateuchal law-codes; the wilderness wanderings.

SECTION 2 — From the Conquest to the Babylonian Exile

The narratives in Joshua, Judges, 1 and 2 Samuel, 1 and 2 Kings; Worship and Holy War.

SECTION 3 — The Preexilic and Exilic Prophets

Introducing the Prophets; Amos; Hosea; Isaiah 1–39; Micah; Jeremiah; Nahum, Habakkuk, Zephaniah; Ezekiel.

SECTION 4 — The Postexilic Period and Judaism

The return from Babylon; the history of the intertestamental period; 1 and 2 Chronicles, Ezra, and Nehemiah; the postexilic prophets; Psalms; Wisdom literature; apocalyptic writings and Daniel, the Apocrypha and Pseudepigrapha; messianic expectations.

SECTION 5 — The Gospels and Acts

First-century Judaism; Mark; Matthew; Luke; John; Acts.

SECTION 6 — The Letters and Revelation

Paul and his letters; the Catholic letters; Revelation

SECTION 1 — From Creation to the Transjordan

CROSS WAYS®

1 SECTION

UNITS 1-10

From Creation to the Transjordan

UNIT 1

The Stage—The Story

A Birdseye View of the Bible Stage and the Biblical Narrative

1A

When asked, "Where do you live?" we usually think of:

- The name of our street and the number of our house;
- The name of the city or town in which we live;
- The state and country in which these are located.

Upper section of **ILLUSTRATION 1A**

This picture, based on photographic images from NASA, invites us to broaden our thinking. It shows a majestic spiral galaxy about 60 million light-years from Planet Earth. A light-year is the distance light travels in a year—approximately six trillion miles (9.6 trillion kilometers). The universe contains tens of billions of such galaxies. Each contains hundreds of billions of stars. The universe is so big that its vastness is impossible to comprehend.

If the Milky Way galaxy, in which our solar system is located, could be seen from a distance, it would look like the galaxy depicted—a giant pinwheel about 100,000 light-years in diameter. It spins around its axis once every 200 million years. The Milky Way galaxy contains about 100 billion stars. To count them at the rate of one per second would take about 3,000 years.

Lower section of **ILLUSTRATION 1A**

This illustration depicts the immediate solar system in which Planet Earth is located. Although the distances between the planets are obviously not to scale, the relative dimensions of the sun and the planets are. To the left is the side of the sun. Flames, thousands of miles long, leap continually from the sun's surface—where the temperature is about 6,000° C (about 11,000° F).

To the right of the sun are the nine planets of our solar system. If the sun were reduced to the size of a beach ball 24 inches (60 centimeters) in diameter, the planets could be represented as follows:

Mercury: a grain of mustard seed 164 feet (50 meters) away

Venus: a pea 284 feet (87 meters) away

Earth: a pea 430 feet (131 meters) away, with the moon a grain of mustard seed 13 feet (4 meters) out from the earth

Mars: a raisin 654 feet (200 meters) away

Jupiter: an orange half a mile (804 meters) away

Saturn: a tangerine four-fifths of a mile (1.3 kilometers) away

Uranus: a plum just over a mile (1.6 kilometers) away

Neptune: a plum over two miles (3.2 kilometers) away

Pluto: a pinhead about three miles (4.8 kilometers) away

The stars and planets in our solar system are relatively small. If the sun were placed at the center of Betelgeuse, a bright red star in the constellation Orion, both Earth and Mars would move around the sun as they do at present distances, and remain within Betelgeuse—which is 431 million miles (694 million kilometers) in diameter. Antares, a double and variable star in the constellation Scorpius and the brightest star in the southern sky, is 522 million miles (840 million kilometers) in diameter.

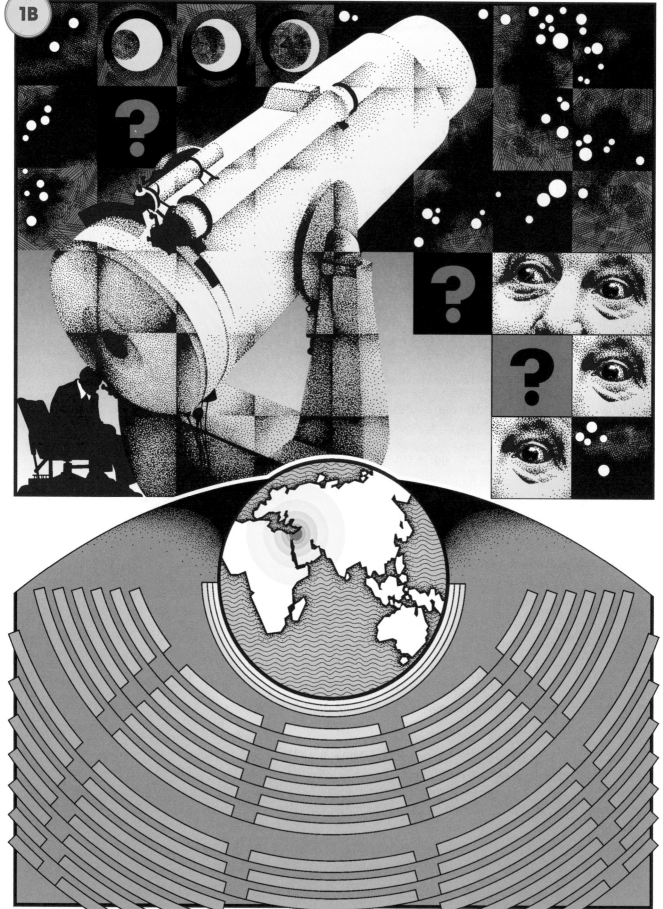

1B

Finding God

Upper section

 A person is peering (**eyes**) through a telescope at a corner of a stylized universe, complete with **phases of the moon**. What he sees moves him to ask many questions (**question marks**).

 How big is the universe? Technology enables astronauts in a space shuttle to orbit the equator at speeds up to 25,000 miles (40,000 kilometers) per hour. However, if people hope to get anywhere in the universe, they must travel at the speed of light, or seven times around the equator in one second. A few years ago scientists said, even at that speed, it would take fourteen billion years to reach the limits of *known* space, which they said was only about one one-billionth of *theoretical* space. Some theorize that outer space is limitless.

3 Although the things seen through telescopes point to God's existence, they do not reveal God's identity and character.

4 We never find God; God is not lost. We are lost, and God finds us. The Bible reveals God as "the hound of heaven" who searches for people to draw them back into fellowship with God and with one another, Genesis 3:8,9; Luke 15:1–10.

Lower section

 This illustration depicts an **amphitheater**, consisting of a **stage** and **seats**. The scenery on the stage is **Planet Earth**—including the **Middle East** where the biblical narrative unfolds. The illustration's message is: God is not merely far off among the stars. Although God is there too, God is everywhere. Telescopes and microscopes reveal God's fingerprints throughout *creation*. However, if we wish to know something about God's heart, character, and disposition we must look elsewhere—to God's involvement in *history*.

2 The Bible teaches that God has made tiny, fragile Planet Earth the special stage for His activities. God's footprints criss-cross all history and provide answers to humanity's questions about life, death, and eternity.

3 The biblical narrative indeed reveals God's involvement in creation and history. However, the more we study that narrative, the more we learn that we are not merely *spectators* watching it happen. We are all *partakers*, totally involved in that narrative—whether we realize it or not, whether we want to or not.

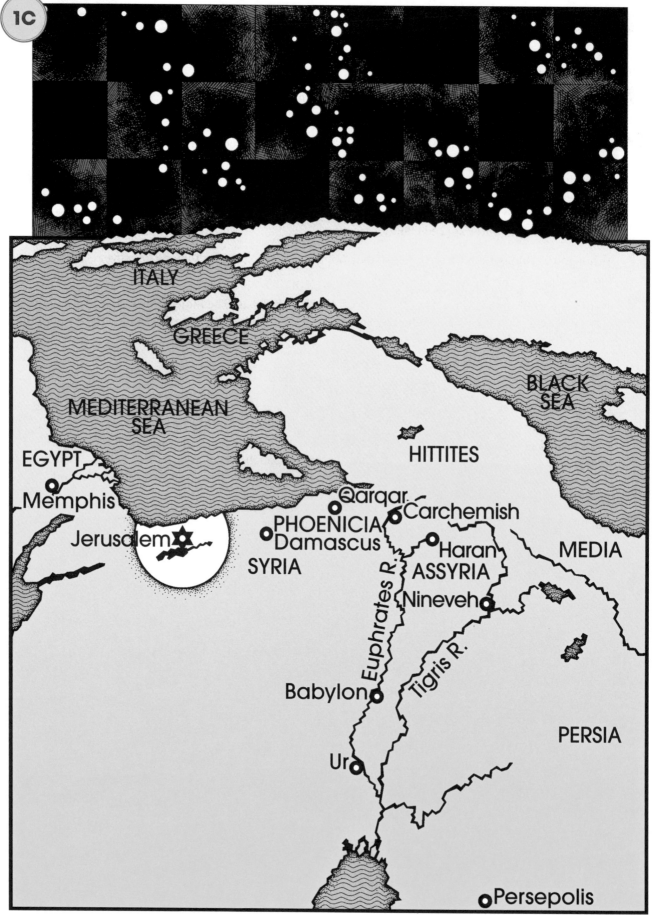

Some think that the ancient Israelites lived in cozy comfort, isolated and insulated from the history of surrounding nations, and devoted themselves to the worship and service of God. Not so! They lived among superpowers that were constantly at war with each other, and they worshiped a variety of gods.

ILLUSTRATION 1C depicts "an astronaut's view" of the **Mediterranean** world in which the biblical narrative unfolds. (*Mediterranean* is derived from two Latin words that mean "in the middle of land.") The land of *Canaan* (**white circle**) is located at "center stage." The *Israelites* who settled in Canaan were the descendants of Abraham, Isaac, and Jacob (later referred to as the *patriarchs*, the *fathers* of the Israelites, the "Chosen People"). David captured **Jerusalem** and made it his capital, 2 Samuel 5:6–10.

There were usually tensions and troubled relations between the Israelites and **SYRIA**. Good relations prevailed between the Israelites and **PHOENICIA**. The Phoenicians were a sea-faring people (the Israelites were not) who played an important role in international trading ventures. The Israelites needed access to their sea-faring skills and services.

The region between the **Tigris** and **Euphrates Rivers** was known as *Mesopotamia*—a name derived from two Greek words meaning "between the rivers."

The *Assyrians*, *Babylonians*, and *Persians* established successive empires in Mesopotamia. The Babylonians conquered Assyrian **Nineveh** in 612 B.C. Cyrus the Persian gained control of **MEDIA** in 550 B.C., and conquered **Babylon** in 539 B.C. The *Greeks* under Alexander the Great ravaged **Persepolis**, a major Persian capital city, in 330 B.C. In 40–37 B.C., the *Parthians* (not shown; to the northeast of Media) helped Antigonus, a descendant of the Jewish Hasmonean rulers (165–63 B.C.), gain control of *Judea* and **Jerusalem**—and block Rome's land-bridge to **EGYPT**. (The Hasmoneans were descendants of the Maccabees who revolted against Antiochus IV "Epiphanes" of Syria in 165 B.C.)

The **HITTITES**, Assyrians, Babylonians, Persians, Greeks, and Romans (**ITALY**) consistently cast covetous eyes on Egypt, whose fertile *Nile Valley* was the bread-basket of the ancient Mediterranean world. When these ancient superpowers set out to plunder Egypt's resources, they marched through Canaan along the way. The Mesopotamian nations could not follow a direct route to Egypt, but had to travel "between the rivers" and down the Mediterranean coast to ensure access to food and water.

The Egyptians were aware of the ambitions and needs of their northern neighbors. To discourage invasions, the Egyptians built a series of fortresses along the Mediterranean coast; the most northern one was located at **Carchemish**. The Egyptians used these fortresses to block the advance of Mesopotamian nations and discourage the empire-building dreams of southern European powers.

Because nations believed that their gods led them into battle and gave them their victories, they usually placed symbols of the gods of conquered nations in their shrines (1 Samuel 5:1,2), and symbols of their gods in the shrines of those they conquered. This practice declared, "Because we were able to conquer you, our gods are obviously stronger than your gods." In 2 Kings 23:4,5 the references to "the host of heaven" and "the sun, the moon, the constellations, and all the host of the heavens" in the Jerusalem Temple are to Assyrian astral deities.

On occasion, God declared that He would use the armies of other nations, such as Assyria and Babylon, to discipline His own rebellious people; see Isaiah 10:5, Jeremiah 27:6.

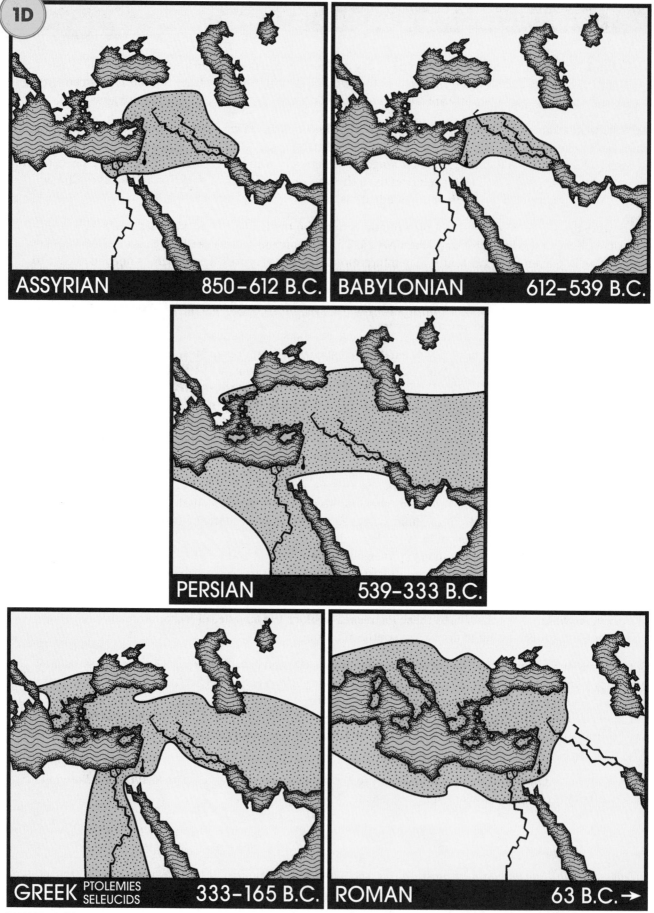

ASSYRIAN 850–612 B.C.

BABYLONIAN 612–539 B.C.

PERSIAN 539–333 B.C.

GREEK PTOLEMIES SELEUCIDS 333–165 B.C.

ROMAN 63 B.C. →

© H. N. Wendt 2006

Memories and Hopes

ILLUSTRATION 1D depicts the five empires that, one after another, took control of ancient Israel and made it part of their empire. The Israelites longed for the day when they would be free of foreign control—and would themselves rule the nations of the world.

① The Assyrian Empire

Assyria was politically active in the Middle East region even before the time of the patriarchs. Fortunately for Israel, Assyrian influence was at its lowest point during the reign of Israel's most popular and powerful king, David (1,000–960 B.C.). In due course, Assyria's power increased, and its influence—particularly in the Northern Kingdom of Israel—resulted in that kingdom becoming an Assyrian vassal in 841 B.C. As Assyria's fortunes and power decreased, Israel and Judah gained some freedom and prominence under Jeroboam II and Uzziah. However, in 745 B.C., Tiglath-Pileser III set about restoring Assyria's imperial state, and dealt harshly with Israelite attempts to gain independence. In 721 B.C., the Assyrians overran the Northern Kingdom of Israel, led its people into exile, and brought its history to an end.

② The Babylonian Empire

The best-known king of the First Babylonian Dynasty (18th century B.C., about the time of Abraham) was Hammurabi, the author of a famous code of laws. During the early part of the first millennium B.C., the Assyrians controlled Babylon. However, the Babylonians threw off the Assyrian yoke in 612 B.C., and dominated the history of Western Asia until 539 B.C. Nebuchadnezzar took thousands of the leading citizens of the Southern Kingdom of Judah into exile in Babylon in two deportations in 597 and 587 B.C.

③ The Persian Empire

The Persians under Cyrus conquered the Babylonians in 539 B.C., and then went on to develop and control an empire stretching from India to the Aegean Sea and Egypt. The Persian rulers treated captive nations much more kindly than the Assyrians and Babylonians had treated them. Eventually their realm became part of the empire of Alexander the Great.

④ The Greek Empire

After Philip of Macedon was assassinated in 336 B.C., his son Alexander, then only 20 years old, succeeded him. By the time of his death in 323 B.C. at the age of 33, Alexander the Great had conquered much of the Mediterranean world. He died during a campaign in Babylon. After his death, several of his generals struggled to gain control of the empire Alexander had established.

Two generals are of importance for understanding Jewish history: Ptolemy and Seleucus. Ptolemy and his descendants (the ***PTOLEMIES***) gained control of Egypt, and ruled Jewish territory 301–198 B.C. Seleucus and his descendants (the ***SELEUCIDS***) ruled Syria, and gained control of Jewish territory in 198 B.C. The Jews, under the leadership of the Maccabees, began a struggle for freedom from the Seleucids in 165 B.C., and finally won full independence in 142 B.C. The Maccabees established a line of Jewish rulers known as the Hasmoneans. The Hasmoneans were not descendants of David.

⑤ The Roman Empire

In 63 B.C., the emperor Pompey made Syria (which included Judah—named Judea by the Romans) a Roman province. The Jewish people remained under Roman control for several centuries. In Jesus' day, the Jews looked for a coming Messiah to deliver them from the Romans. However, the New Testament writers point out that the Romans did not constitute the "real enemy," Matthew 1:21; Mark 3:27.

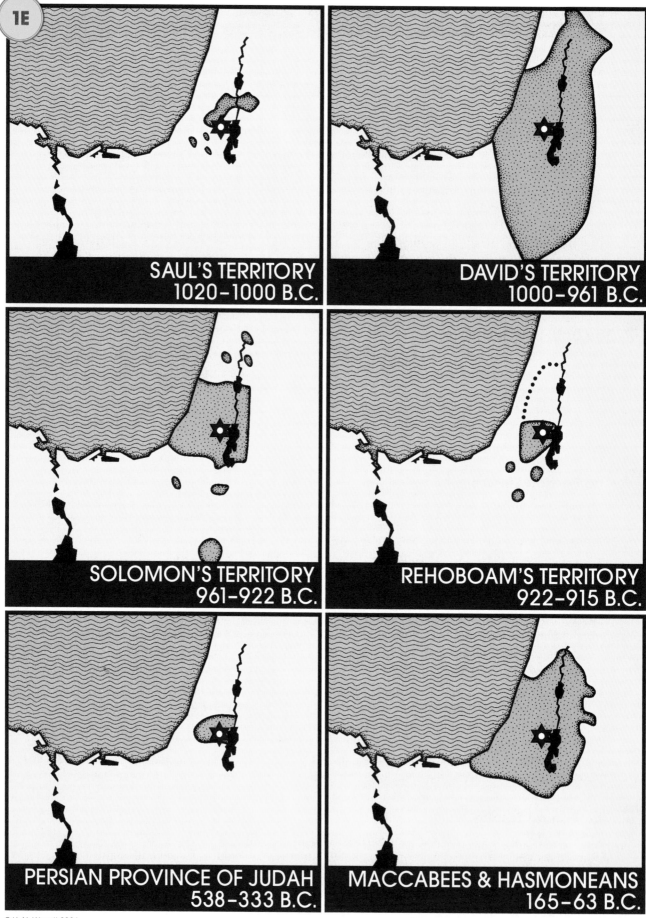

1E

SAUL'S TERRITORY
1020–1000 B.C.

DAVID'S TERRITORY
1000–961 B.C.

SOLOMON'S TERRITORY
961–922 B.C.

REHOBOAM'S TERRITORY
922–915 B.C.

PERSIAN PROVINCE OF JUDAH
538–333 B.C.

MACCABEES & HASMONEANS
165–63 B.C.

ILLUSTRATION 1E shows how Israel's borders increased and decreased as its fortunes waxed and waned during the first millennium B.C. The postexilic community hoped that God would one day make their realm as large as David's kingdom had been, Mark 11:10.

 Saul's Territory

The size of the territory that Saul ruled is uncertain. Although many believe that Saul's kingdom was quite small, 1 Samuel 14:47,48 reports that he carried out numerous punitive campaigns against neighboring nations that had harassed the Israelites. However, this passage does not state that he incorporated these regions into his realm.

② David's Territory

David's realm was large. Memories of its size continued to influence the Jewish people throughout their history, and gave rise to the Zealot revolts against the Romans in A.D. 66–70 and 132–135.

③ Solomon's Territory

First Kings 4:21 suggests that Solomon's realm was even larger than David's. However, toward the close of Solomon's reign, his realm decreased in size when the Syrians and Edomites gained their independence, 1 Kings 11:14–25.

④ Rehoboam's Territory

Solomon's son, Rehoboam, gained control only of the regions of Judah and Benjamin, 1 Kings 12:21. The Northern Kingdom was taken over by Jeroboam (1 Kings 11:26–40; 12:1–33) and ruled by nine different dynasties. The Assyrians destroyed it in 721 B.C. After revolts against Babylon by King Jehoiakim and King Zedekiah, many from Judah were taken into exile in Babylon in 597 and 587 B.C. A year after the Persians conquered Babylon in 539 B.C., many of the exiles began to return to Judah.

 Postexilic Judah

While under the control of first the Persians and then the Greeks, postexilic Judah was small. Apart from a short period under the Maccabees and their descendants, the Hasmoneans, it was never independent.

⑥ Maccabees and Hasmoneans

The Maccabees (later known as the Hasmoneans) revolted against the Syrian Seleucids in 165 B.C. They gained full independence in 142 B.C., and established a realm of considerable size—which some saw as the Messianic Kingdom. The Hasmonean rulers angered many when they assumed the role of High Priest. Although they were Levites (the priestly tribe descended from Aaron, a Levite), they were not descendants of David's priest, Zadok. (*It was believed that only a descendant of Zadok could be a legitimate High Priest.* Zadok anointed Solomon as David's successor, 1 Kings 1:32–48; note 1 Chronicles 15:11 and the many references to Zadok throughout 1 and 2 Chronicles; see Ezekiel 40:46, 43:19, 44:15, 48:11.) The level of anger increased when the Hasmonean ruler combined the role of *High Priest* with that of *king. Only descendants of David could be legitimate kings!* In **63 B.C.**, the Romans forcibly took control of Judah, and Hasmonean rule ended.

For hundreds of years, many within Judaism continued to hope that one day God would restore the Davidic kingdom. Up to the very moment of Jesus' ascension, even His disciples shared that hope, Acts 1:6.

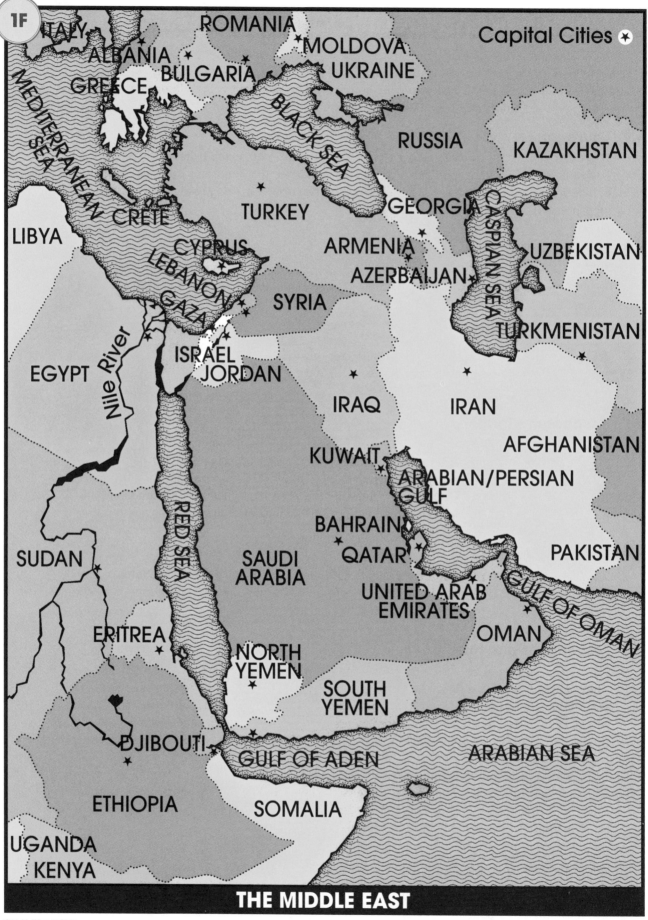

1F Capital Cities ✱

ITALY
ALBANIA
GREECE
BULGARIA
ROMANIA
MOLDOVA
UKRAINE
MEDITERRANEAN SEA
BLACK SEA
RUSSIA
KAZAKHSTAN
CRETE
TURKEY
GEORGIA
CASPIAN SEA
LIBYA
CYPRUS
ARMENIA
AZERBAIJAN
UZBEKISTAN
LEBANON
GAZA
SYRIA
TURKMENISTAN
Nile River
ISRAEL
JORDAN
EGYPT
IRAQ
IRAN
AFGHANISTAN
KUWAIT
RED SEA
ARABIAN/PERSIAN GULF
SUDAN
SAUDI ARABIA
BAHRAIN
QATAR
PAKISTAN
UNITED ARAB EMIRATES
OMAN
GULF OF OMAN
ERITREA
NORTH YEMEN
SOUTH YEMEN
DJIBOUTI
GULF OF ADEN
ARABIAN SEA
ETHIOPIA
SOMALIA
UGANDA
KENYA

THE MIDDLE EAST

ILLUSTRATION 1F shows the part of the world in which most of the events recorded in the biblical narrative took place. However, the borders shown are those in place today.

The location of the capital city of each country is marked with a *five-pointed star*. According to the United Nations, the capital of Israel is Tel Aviv; according to Israeli leaders, it is Jerusalem.

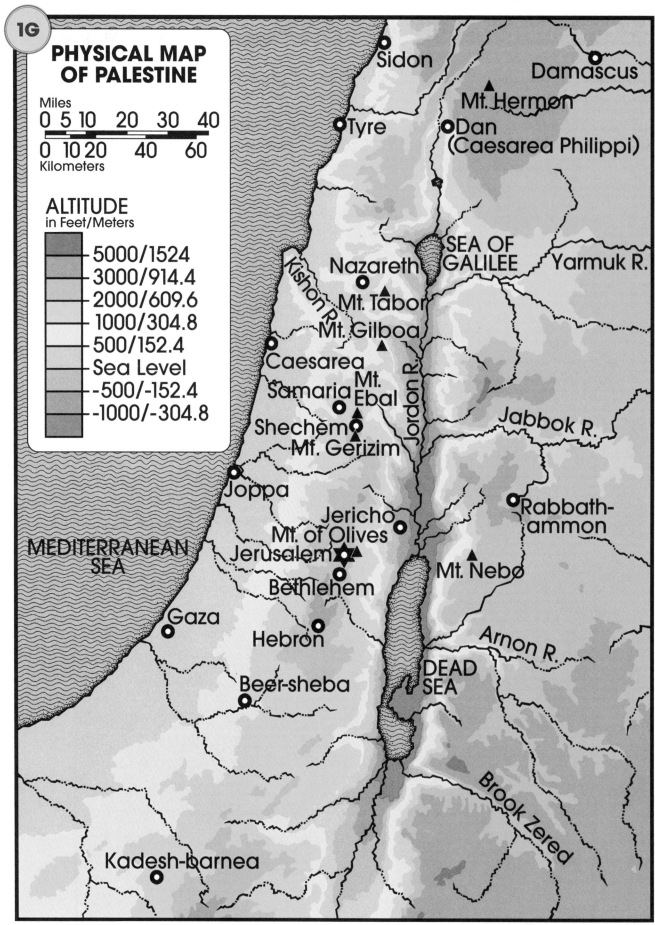

PHYSICAL MAP OF PALESTINE

Miles
0 5 10 20 30 40

0 10 20 40 60
Kilometers

ALTITUDE
in Feet/Meters

5000/1524
3000/914.4
2000/609.6
1000/304.8
500/152.4
Sea Level
-500/-152.4
-1000/-304.8

Sidon

Damascus

Mt. Hermon

Tyre

Dan
(Caesarea Philippi)

Kishon R.

Nazareth

SEA OF
GALILEE

Yarmuk R.

Mt. Tabor

Mt. Gilboa

Caesarea

Mt.
Ebal

Samaria

Jordan R.

Jabbok R.

Shechem

Mt. Gerizim

Joppa

Rabbath-
ammon

Jericho

Mt. of Olives

Jerusalem

Mt. Nebo

MEDITERRANEAN
SEA

Bethlehem

Gaza

Hebron

Arnon R.

Beer-sheba

DEAD
SEA

Brook Zered

Kadesh-barnea

© H. N. Wendt 2006

ILLUSTRATION 1G contains information about the height above and below sea level of various parts of what today is still referred to as the Holy Land. It also locates some of the seas, cities, towns, rivers, and mountains that are mentioned in the biblical narrative.

1 The Israelites spent many years in the vicinity of **Kadesh-barnea** during their time in the wilderness, Numbers 20:1; 32:8.

2 As they approach the **DEAD SEA**, the **Arnon River** and **Brook Zered** become large canyons, or wadis.

3 **Rabbath-ammon** is present-day Amman, the capital of Jordan.

4 Just before he died, Moses stood on **Mt. Nebo** and was granted the joy of looking across the **Jordan River** to view the land of Canaan, Deuteronomy 34:1–5.

5 Melting snow from **Mt. Hermon** provides most of the water for the **Jordan River**.

6 The **SEA OF GALILEE** is about 635 feet (192 meters) below sea level. The **Jordan River** makes many twists and turns as it makes its way south from the Sea of Galilee to the **DEAD SEA**—which is about 1,300 feet below sea level (396 meters) and contains a high percentage of salt. No fish live within its waters.

7 **Beer-sheba** played a role in the lives of Abraham, Isaac, and Jacob; Genesis 31:25–34; 26:23–25; 46:5.

8 King Saul committed suicide on **Mt. Gilboa**, 1 Samuel 31:1–7.

9 King David was born in **Bethlehem**, 1 Samuel 16:1–13. So was Jesus the Messiah, Luke 2:1–7.

10 David's *first* capital city was **Hebron**, 2 Samuel 1–4; his *second*, **Jerusalem**, 2 Samuel 5:6–10.

11 **Mt. Gerizim** (Deuteronomy 27:11–14) eventually became the holy mountain for the Samaritans.

12 **Samaria** became the capital city for the Northern Kingdom, 1 Kings 16:24.

13 **Damascus** was (and remains) the capital of Syria, 1 Kings 11:24.

14 After Rome gained control of Judah, its governing officials resided in **Caesarea**, Acts 23:33.

15 Jesus grew up in **Nazareth**, Matthew 2:21–23; Luke 2:39,40.

16 Jesus revealed the nature of His Messiahship on the way to **Caesarea Philippi** (previously known as **Dan**), Mark 8:27–38.

17 At **Jericho**, Jesus healed a blind man (Luke 18:35–43) and dined with Zacchaeus, a tax-collector, Luke 19:1–10.

18 On Palm Sunday, Jesus stood on the **Mount of Olives** on the eastern edge of **Jerusalem**, and looked across the Kidron Valley to the city where He would be crucified, Matthew 21:1–11.

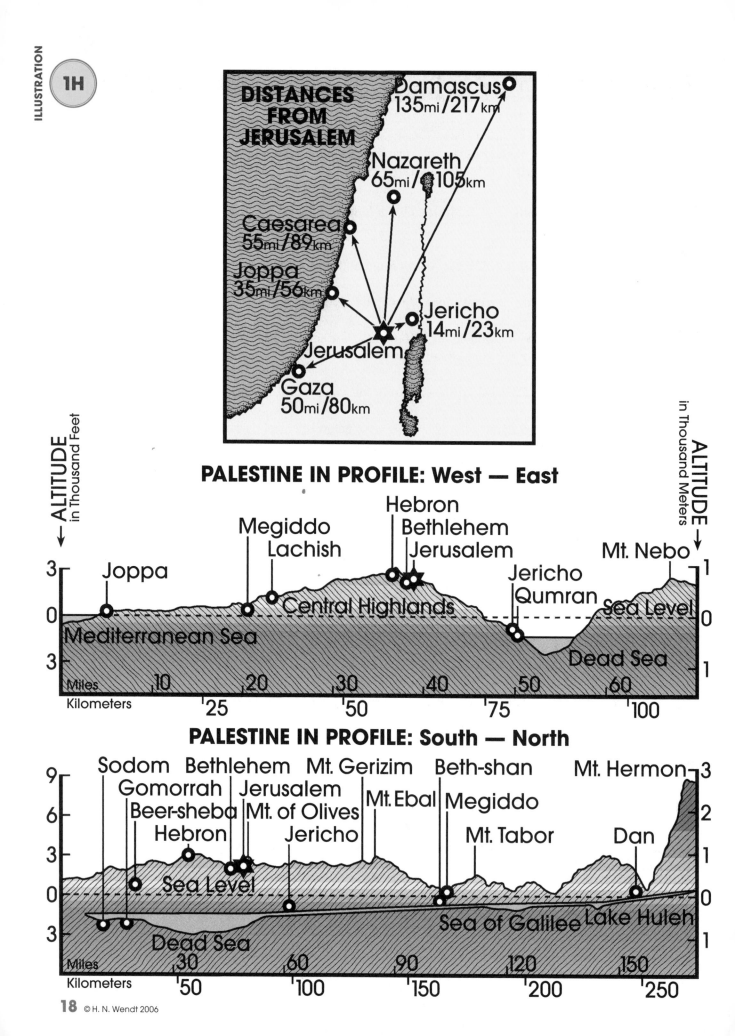

DISTANCES FROM JERUSALEM

Damascus 135mi /217km

Nazareth 65mi /105km

Caesarea 55mi /89km

Joppa 35mi /56km

Jericho 14mi /23km

Jerusalem

Gaza 50mi /80km

PALESTINE IN PROFILE: West — East

ALTITUDE in Thousand Feet

ALTITUDE in Thousand Meters

Hebron
Bethlehem
Jerusalem

Megiddo
Lachish

Mt. Nebo

Joppa

Jericho
Qumran

Central Highlands

Sea Level

Mediterranean Sea

Dead Sea

Miles 10 20 30 40 50 60
Kilometers 25 50 75 100

PALESTINE IN PROFILE: South — North

Sodom
Gomorrah
Beer-sheba
Hebron

Bethlehem
Jerusalem
Mt. of Olives
Jericho

Mt. Gerizim
Mt. Ebal

Beth-shan
Megiddo
Mt. Tabor

Mt. Hermon

Dan

Sea Level

Dead Sea

Sea of Galilee Lake Huleh

Miles 30 60 90 120 150
Kilometers 50 100 150 200 250

Palestine in Profile

1H

Upper section

The distances in miles and kilometers from ***Jerusalem*** to several neighboring cities.

Middle section

The profile of ***PALESTINE*** from west to east.

- The ***Dead Sea*** is the lowest place on earth.
- Some ancient Israelites believed that ***Jerusalem*** was on earth's highest hill. They spoke of going *up* to Jerusalem, and *down* from Jerusalem.
- Just prior to his death, Moses stood on Mt. Nebo to have a panoramic view of the Promised Land, Deuteronomy 34:1–5.

Lower section

The profile of ***PALESTINE*** from south to north.

Because the details in the middle and lower illustrations are compressed, the mountains appear much steeper than they actually are. Even so, the topography of that small country referred to as the Holy Land is very rugged.

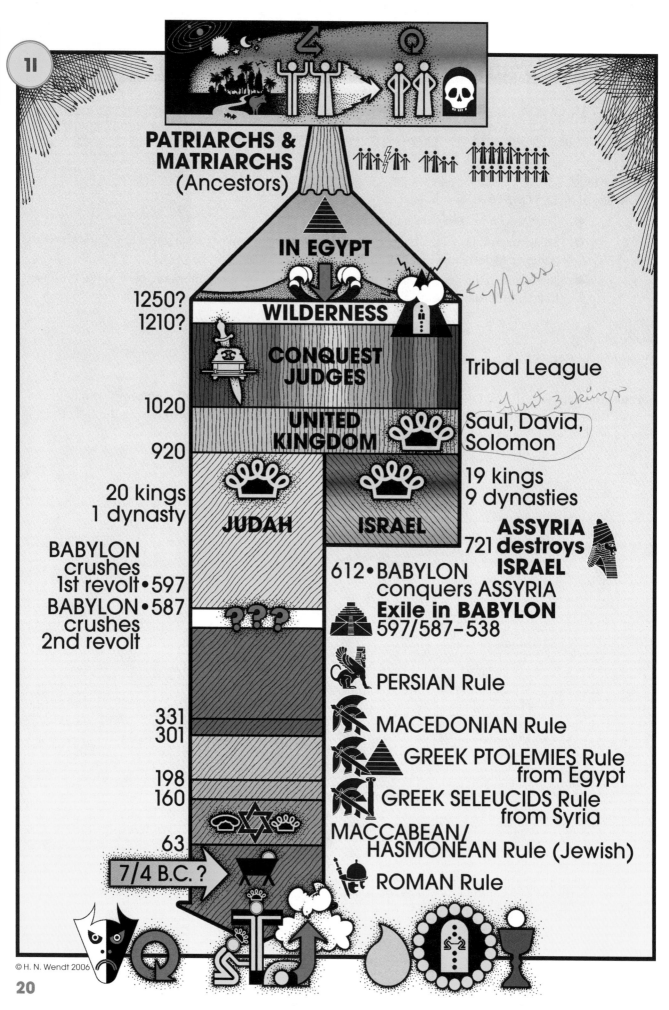

11

**PATRIARCHS &
MATRIARCHS**
(Ancestors)

IN EGYPT

1250?
1210?

WILDERNESS

← Moses

**CONQUEST
JUDGES**

Tribal League

1020

**UNITED
KINGDOM**

first 3 kings

Saul, David,
Solomon

920

20 kings
1 dynasty

JUDAH

ISRAEL

19 kings
9 dynasties

**ASSYRIA
destroys
ISRAEL**

721

BABYLON
crushes
1st revolt • 597

BABYLON • 587
crushes
2nd revolt

612 • **BABYLON**
conquers ASSYRIA

Exile in BABYLON
597/587–538

???

PERSIAN Rule

331
301

MACEDONIAN Rule

GREEK PTOLEMIES Rule
from Egypt

198
160

GREEK SELEUCIDS Rule
from Syria

MACCABEAN/
HASMONEAN Rule (Jewish)

63

7/4 B.C. ?

ROMAN Rule

The Biblical Narrative—a Birdseye View

ILLUSTRATION 1I presents an overview of the biblical narrative, which deals with the rise and fall of a succession of empires and kingdoms—until the one, true, eternal Kingdom of God breaks into human history through the mind, manner, message, mission, and ministry of Jesus the Messiah.

THE OLD TESTAMENT NARRATIVE AND MESSAGE

1 The rectangular box at the top of **ILLUSTRATION 1I** contains the following symbols:

- *Solar system, trees, birds, fish, animals:* Genesis 1:1–2:25 outline God's actions in creating the universe, Planet Earth, birds, animals, and fish.
- *Male and female figures with arms raised in praise to God; double-headed arrow above them:* God created humanity's parents. They were to live to serve God and each other.
- *Male and female figures with hands on hips, circular arrow above them; tombstone with skull:* People sinned. They sought to do *their* will (serve self) rather than *God's* will (serve God by serving others). The result was death for humanity.

2 *PATRIARCHS & MATRIARCHS:* The narratives in Genesis 12–50 tell how God formed a people to carry out a mission to draw humanity back into fellowship with God and each other. The *figures to the right of the line descending from the upper illustration* represent:

- Abraham, Sarah, Isaac/Hagar, Ishmael;
- Isaac, Rebekah, Esau, Jacob;
- Jacob, his two wives and two concubines, his twelve sons and one daughter.

3 *IN EGYPT:* The closing chapters of Genesis tell us why and how Jacob and his clan (now called the Israelites) moved from Canaan to Egypt (*pyramid*) where they lived for several hundred years. Jacob's son, Joseph, plays a central role in this narrative. The Bible says little about the history of Jacob and his descendants after they settled in Egypt. Exodus 1:8 states that Abraham's descendants were eventually enslaved by a pharaoh "who did not know Joseph." However, God rescued the Israelites from the power of the Pharaoh by *opening up the waters* to enable them to escape from Egypt (*arrow passing through open waters*).

4 *WILDERNESS:* God led the Israelites into the wilderness of the Sinai Peninsula where they lived for forty years. After revealing His presence in the form of *cloud and lightning at the top of Mount Sinai* (Exodus 19), God made a *covenant* (Exodus 20:1–21) with His people. This covenant contained *six sections*, the third consisting of the *commandments*.

5 *CONQUEST, JUDGES: The Ark of the Covenant*, signifying God's presence, made it possible for the Israelites to cross the River Jordan into Canaan (Joshua 3). After entering the Promised Land, the Israelites, under the leadership of Joshua, engaged in a Holy War (*sword*) in an attempt to rid the land of the Canaanites. After settling in Canaan, the Israelites formed a *Tribal League*, a loose confederation of tribes, and were ruled by leaders referred to as "judges." The tribal league faced three major problems:

- Political disunity;
- Dynastic uncertainty;
- Spiritual syncretism (i.e., worshiping false gods as well as the true and only God).

6 *UNITED KINGDOM:* The people sought to deal with the first two problems by appointing *Saul* of Benjamin as king (*crown*), and then by establishing a line of kings beginning with *David* (from the tribe of Judah), who was followed by his son *Solomon*.

7 *JUDAH/ISRAEL:* After Solomon's death, the nation divided. The Southern Kingdom was called *JUDAH*; the Northern Kingdom was called *ISRAEL*. Eventually, the Assyrians conquered Israel and made it part of their empire. When Israel sought freedom, the Assyrians destroyed it in *721* B.C. Although they did not destroy Judah, they made it part of their realm.

8 *JUDAH; Exile in BABYLON:* Eventually the Babylonians conquered the Assyrians, and incorporated their territory (including Judah) into their empire. Nebuchadnezzar of Babylon put down a revolt in Judah in *597* B.C. When Judah revolted again, Nebuchadnezzar destroyed Judah, Jerusalem, and its Temple in *587* B.C. After both campaigns, Nebuchadnezzar took thousands of Judah's leading citizens into *Exile in BABYLON*. Those who experienced the exile in Babylon asked *many questions* about why the tragedy happened, and what the future would bring. They prayed to God to take vengeance on the Babylonians (Psalm 137).

9 *PERSIAN Rule:* Cyrus the Persian gained control of Babylon in 539 B.C., and in *538* permitted the Jewish exiles to return to Judah and Jerusalem, and to rebuild the Temple. Even so, Judah was not given political freedom but remained a Persian province. Because the two Judean kings taken to Babylon in *597* and *587* B.C. died during the exile, the Davidic dynasty was no more.

10 *MACEDONIAN, GREEK PTOLEMIES, GREEK SELEUCIDS Rule:* The *MACEDONIAN* Greeks overthrew the Persians in *331* B.C. After the death of Alexander the Great in 323 B.C., the *PTOLEMIES* (Egypt-based Greek rulers) ruled Judah until *198* B.C., when the *SELEUCIDS* (Syria-based Greek rulers) gained control of Judah.

11 *MACCABEAN/HASMONEAN Rule:* The Jews (under the leadership of Judas Maccabeus) began fighting to gain freedom from Seleucid rule in 167 B.C., cleansed and rededicated the Temple in 164 B.C., gained full political independence in 142 B.C., and from then until *63* B.C. were ruled by descendants of the Maccabees known as the *Hasmoneans*. Some Hasmonean rulers were viewed with disfavor by many in Judah. They combined the office of *High Priest* (*priest's headdress*) with that of *king* (*crown*), although they were not descendants of either David's priest Zadok or of David (*star of David*). Furthermore, some Hasmoneans were ready to embrace Greek religious and cultural practices (*Hellenism*), and treated their subjects harshly and cruelly.

12 *ROMAN Rule:* The Romans took control of Judah in *63* B.C.

Throughout the postexilic period, many Jewish people longed for political freedom and the restoration of David's dynasty and kingdom.

THE NEW TESTAMENT NARRATIVE AND MESSAGE
The mission and ministry of Jesus the Messiah

Row of symbols at the *bottom* of **ILLUSTRATION 11**:

The Davidic dynasty was restored in an unexpected manner when Jesus of Nazareth, a descendant of David, was born (*manger*) in Bethlehem, David's birthplace. Precisely in what year Jesus was born is uncertain (*7/4 B.C. ? within arrow*).

1. Jesus the Messiah ("anointed one") lived the life of a servant-without-limit—even to the point of giving away life on a cross (**crowned Jesus in servant posture**; **crowned Jesus on a cross**). The nature of Jesus' kingship and kingdom was radically different from the hopes of the Jewish people.

2. Jesus conquered the power of death, and returned to life on Easter Sunday morning (**open tomb**). The empty tomb is God's affirmation of Jesus' kingship.

3. Jesus' action in ascending (**rising red arrow**) into a **cloud** did not mean that He departed from Planet Earth for some distant corner of the universe. In the ascension, Jesus did not *withdraw* His presence but *transformed* it. Jesus, God's Living Word, *remains among us invisibly*. We, His people, wait for Him to *reappear* on the Final Day of history.

4. The Holy Spirit (**dove**) continues to make Jesus' completed saving work known to humanity through God's written and spoken Word.

5. **Satanic face; symbol for sin:** Jesus proclaimed that humanity's real enemy was not Rome, nor any political regime, past or present. It was (*and is!*) the Satanic—every spirit, power, person, pressure, and institution that seeks to sidetrack people from living to serve God and others into serving themselves.

6. **Large circle of small circles around a symbol for God's "new covenant":** God's will, revealed in Jesus, the Living Word, is that His people live *in community*—with no concern for borders, flags, or skin color—serving each other in the spirit and manner of Jesus, their forgiving Savior and servant Lord (**two figures facing each other in servant posture at position "3" in the new covenant**). Jesus gives His brothers and sisters only *one* commandment—that they love and serve each other in the spirit of their Heavenly Brother, John 13:1–15. All other commandments referred to in the New Testament writings serve as commentaries on Jesus' one commandment.

7. **Drop of water** (Holy Baptism)**:** When people are baptized, they are made "sharers in" Jesus' sinless life, death for sin, experience of the grave, and victory over death, Romans 6:1–11. They are adopted into God's eternal family. Throughout life, they are to seek to reflect the mind and manner of their Brother, Jesus the Messiah.

8. **Bread and cup** (Lord's Supper)**:** In Jesus' day (and still today in Middle Eastern understanding), those who eat together declare themselves to be family. They pledge themselves to defend each other with their very lives. They can never again refer disparagingly to the sins and failings of those with whom they eat and drink. They are to seek only to edify and serve each other, and help each other reflect the mind and manner of Jesus as they live out life in caring community.

In the early church, when Augustine of Hippo (A.D.354–430) celebrated the Lord's Supper, he pointed to the sacred elements on the altar and said, "Behold, the body of Christ." Next, he pointed to the members of the congregation and said, "And you are the body of Christ." He would then say to those present, "Come, eat what you are. Go forth to become what you eat."

When people today participate in the Lord's Supper, they are to bear in mind that many millions of people in many countries around the world are participating in the same meal on the same day. All participants belong to God's family of forgiven saints, and all are to devote life to praising God and serving each other in the spirit of Jesus, their forgiving Savior and Servant Lord. In their prayer life, they are to focus on what God has done for them and what God desires of them.

1A We humans live:

- on a tiny planet,
- in a huge solar system,
- in a vast galaxy,
- in an infinite universe.

1B When we look through a telescope, we see something of the grandeur of God's creation. Although what we see tells us something about God's power, it does not tell us anything about God's involvement in human history. To understand that phenomenon, we must study the storyline that runs through the Old and New Testaments. The stage for that storyline is what today we refer to as the Middle East—in particular the territory referred to as Palestine, Israel, the Promised Land, and the Holy Land.

1C The Promised Land was situated in a strategic location in the biblical Mediterranean world with ancient superpowers to its south, northeast, and northwest.

1D With the passing of the centuries, the land came under the control of the following powers:

- Assyria
- Babylon
- Persia
- Greece
- Rome

1E As the history of God's Old Testament people unfolded, the size of their territory waxed and waned. Its borders were at their greatest size during the reign of David. Prior to the Romans taking control in 63 B.C., the Maccabees and Hasmoneans extended its borders to almost what they had been at the time of David.

1F Today's map of the Middle East is very different from that of biblical times. Even so, as a result of events that took place during the past century, the land of Israel continues to play a strategic role in Middle Eastern and world events.

1G The land of Israel has remarkable features. The Sea of Galilee is about 630 feet (192 meters) below sea level; the Dead Sea is about 1,300 feet (396 meters) below sea level. Some parts of Israel are fertile and beautiful; others are rugged and arid. The highest peak within the land is a little less than 3,000 feet (914 meters).

1H The land of Israel is small—about 150 miles (240 kilometers) long and 50 miles (80 kilometers) wide. Disputes continue as to what belongs to Israel, and what belongs to the Palestinians and neighboring countries.

1I The biblical narrative deals with the rise and fall of a succession of empires and kingdoms—until the one, true, eternal Kingdom of God broke into human history through the ministry, mission, message, mind, and manner of Jesus the Messiah.

CROSS WAYS®

1
SECTION

UNITS 1–10

From Creation to the Transjordan

UNIT 2
God's Book—God's Plan

The structure of the Bible and an overview of God's plan for humanity

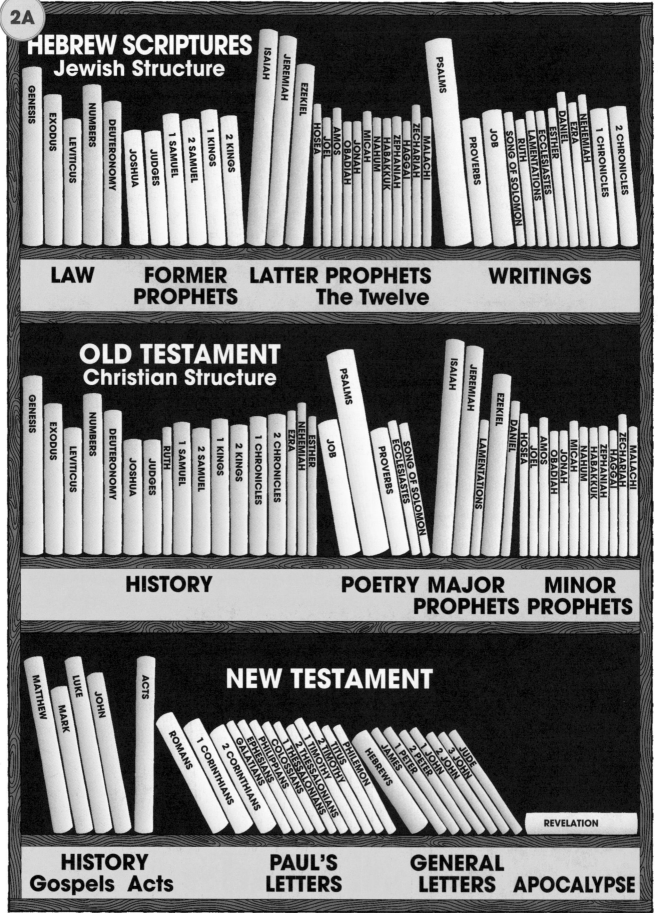

HEBREW SCRIPTURES
Jewish Structure

GENESIS · EXODUS · LEVITICUS · NUMBERS · DEUTERONOMY · JOSHUA · JUDGES · 1 SAMUEL · 2 SAMUEL · 1 KINGS · 2 KINGS · ISAIAH · JEREMIAH · EZEKIEL · HOSEA · JOEL · AMOS · OBADIAH · JONAH · MICAH · NAHUM · HABAKKUK · ZEPHANIAH · HAGGAI · ZECHARIAH · MALACHI · PSALMS · PROVERBS · JOB · SONG OF SOLOMON · RUTH · LAMENTATIONS · ECCLESIASTES · ESTHER · DANIEL · EZRA · NEHEMIAH · 1 CHRONICLES · 2 CHRONICLES

LAW · FORMER PROPHETS · LATTER PROPHETS The Twelve · WRITINGS

OLD TESTAMENT
Christian Structure

GENESIS · EXODUS · LEVITICUS · NUMBERS · DEUTERONOMY · JOSHUA · JUDGES · RUTH · 1 SAMUEL · 2 SAMUEL · 1 KINGS · 2 KINGS · 1 CHRONICLES · 2 CHRONICLES · EZRA · NEHEMIAH · ESTHER · JOB · PSALMS · PROVERBS · ECCLESIASTES · SONG OF SOLOMON · ISAIAH · JEREMIAH · LAMENTATIONS · EZEKIEL · DANIEL · HOSEA · JOEL · AMOS · OBADIAH · JONAH · MICAH · NAHUM · HABAKKUK · ZEPHANIAH · HAGGAI · ZECHARIAH · MALACHI

HISTORY · POETRY MAJOR PROPHETS MINOR PROPHETS

NEW TESTAMENT

MATTHEW · MARK · LUKE · JOHN · ACTS · ROMANS · 1 CORINTHIANS · 2 CORINTHIANS · GALATIANS · EPHESIANS · PHILIPPIANS · COLOSSIANS · 1 THESSALONIANS · 2 THESSALONIANS · 1 TIMOTHY · 2 TIMOTHY · TITUS · PHILEMON · HEBREWS · JAMES · 1 PETER · 2 PETER · 1 JOHN · 2 JOHN · 3 JOHN · JUDE · REVELATION

HISTORY Gospels Acts · PAUL'S LETTERS · GENERAL LETTERS · APOCALYPSE

© H. N. Wendt 2006

The Greek word *byblos*, from which the English word "Bible" is derived, means "book." However, the Bible is really a **library of books** written by numerous authors over hundreds of years. **ILLUSTRATION 2A** depicts three shelves of books.

1 The **first shelf** contains the books that make up the **HEBREW SCRIPTURES**, and shows how they are grouped. The Jewish people refer to:

- Genesis through Deuteronomy as the *Torah* (or **LAW**, *Instruction*, *Teaching*). The Torah deals with the origin and mission of the ancient Israelites, and how they are to live.

- Joshua, Judges, 1 and 2 Samuel, 1 and 2 Kings as the **FORMER PROPHETS**, and Isaiah, Jeremiah, Ezekiel, and Hosea through Malachi as the **LATTER PROPHETS**. Jewish teachers refer to the prophetic writings as the *Nebi'im*.

  The *Former Prophets* describe how the Israelites forsook their God-given mission, worshiped other gods, and eventually were taken into exile to Assyria and Babylon.

  The *Latter Prophets* consist of the writings of Israel's ancient prophets who warned the people that they were ignoring God's goodness and will for their lives, and that tragedy would overtake them if they did not repent and return to the God of their fathers.

- The rest of the books as the **WRITINGS** (or *Kethubim*). Some of the Writings describe how the exiles who returned from Babylon reestablished themselves and their Jerusalem-based worship system. Some are Wisdom writings. The Psalms were used in worship.

The Jewish religious community refers to its Bible as **TaNaK**, a word made up of the first letters in *Torah*, *Nebi'im*, and *Kethubim*. Christian scholars generally consider the Jewish arrangement of the Old Testament books more appropriate.

2 The **second shelf** contains the **OLD TESTAMENT** books in Bibles used by Protestants, and the order in which they are placed in those Bibles.

3 The **third shelf** contains the **NEW TESTAMENT** books used by Protestants and Roman Catholics.

The *Roman Catholic* and *Orthodox Churches* add a number of books to what they consider to be the canon of Scripture. These are generally referred to as the *Apocryphal* or *Deuterocanonical* books. Many Bibles used by Protestants also contain these books. They contain information about the history and faith of the Jewish people during the period *between the Testaments*.

- *The Roman Catholic Old Testament Canon* contains the following additional writings; Tobit, Judith, Six Additions to Esther, 1 Maccabees, 2 Maccabees, Wisdom of Solomon, Ecclesiasticus (Sirach), Baruch (ch. 6, The Letter of Jeremiah), Three Additions to Daniel (The Prayer of Azariah and the Song of the Three Young Men, Susanna, Bel and the Dragon).

- *The Orthodox Old Testament Canon* contains the same additional writings as the Roman Catholic Canon, plus Psalm 151, Lamentations of Jeremiah, Epistle of Jeremiah.

- *Greek Orthodox Bibles* also contain 4 Maccabees and the Prayer of Manasseh. *Slavonic Bibles* add these two writings plus 3 Esdras.

2B

Personality Hats

Let's imagine we are watching a woman buying a hat in a store. The assistant spends half an hour showing her a variety of styles. Finally, the assistant places one on her client's head and says, "Perfect! It's you!"—suggesting that the hat reflects the wearer's personality.

Similarly, in their imaginations, people put a variety of *personality hats* on God. **ILLUSTRATION 2B** depicts some of those "hats."

1. *Graduate's hat:* God knows everything, John 21:17.

2. *Policeman's hat:* God is always out to catch and punish sinners, Genesis 3:8–10.

3. *Chef's hat:* God supplies daily bread, Psalm 145:15,16.

4. *Father Christmas* or *Santa Claus hat:* Many think that it is God's job to provide an endless supply of gifts and favors to make life pleasant, Deuteronomy 28:1–14; Isaiah 3:18–23.

5. *Magician's hat:* God is the great miracle worker, Exodus 7–10.

6. *Crown:* God is King of the universe, Psalm 24:1,2,7–10.

7. *Puritan's hat:* God wants people to work hard, and perhaps be a little stern, Mark 10:17–22.

8. *Doctor's headgear:* God can and should heal people when they are sick, Psalm 103:3.

Although there is an element of truth in each of these "hats" as they relate to God's character, the next illustration introduces us to a hat that Jesus once wore—and to a symbol that depicts God's character in a way that reflects biblical teaching.

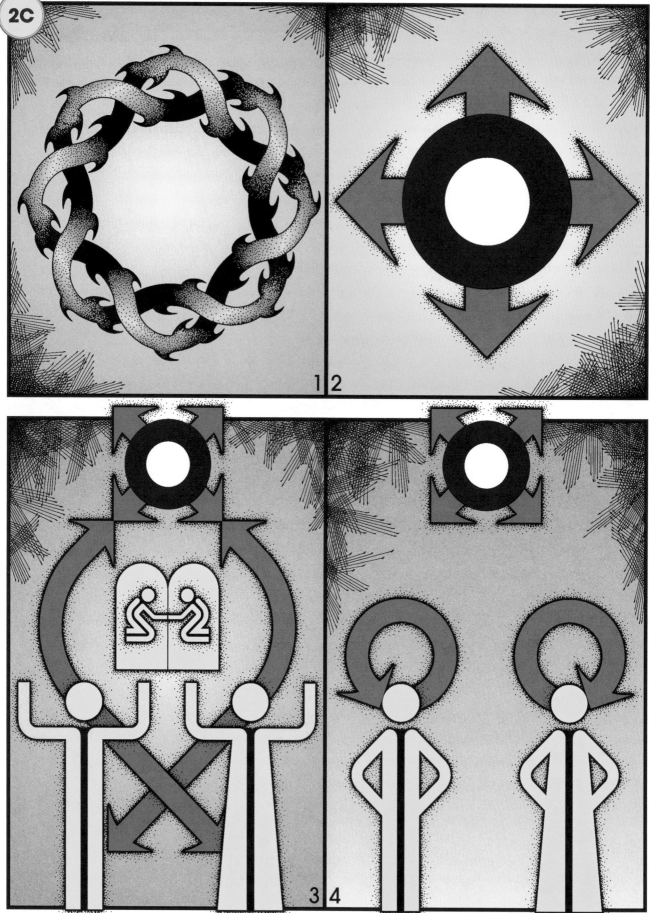

Upper section

1 God once wore a hat (*a crown of thorns*) when, in the person of Jesus the Messiah, He was crucified. A crown of thorns is *circular. Thorns protrude from it.* This hat becomes the basis for the symbol for God introduced in segment 2—a circle with four arrows protruding from it.

2 The **circle** expresses the truth that *God is one* and has *no beginning and no end.* The **arrows** signify that God is always *One who acts,* that the key quality to God's actions is *love,* and that this love always goes *out* from God. God is like a tank full of love, kindness, and mercy—a tank whose faucet is always turned on, and whose contents always flow out and never stop.

Lower section

3 God made people to reflect His behavior pattern, to be "in His image," to be creatures who *love.* Their love is to flow *out* to **God** and to **others**. Love of God expresses itself in service to others.

    a. The Old Testament quotes the first commandment (to love God) in Deuteronomy 6:4,5 and the second (to love neighbor) in Leviticus 19:18. In Jesus' day, most Jewish teachers looked on these as two separate commandments.

    b. Jesus welds these *two* commandments into *one,* Mark 12:28–31; Matthew 22:34–40. Those who love God demonstrate it by loving (serving) others full-time. *Serving* has to do with developing and using life to benefit others.

    c. In the parable of the Good Samaritan (Luke 10:25–37), Jesus deals with a person who:

        ● looks on obedience as a *merit system,* and

        ● wants to *place limits* on who the neighbor is, and how far we are to go in serving that neighbor.

    Jesus teaches that:

        ● the commandments were never meant to serve as a merit system, and

        ● there are to be no limits as to who the neighbor is and how far we are to go in serving that neighbor. The question is not merely "Who *is* my neighbor?" but rather "What does it mean to *be* a neighbor?"

    In this parable, the priest and the Levite walked past the helpless (*possibly* dead) victim of robbers because they asked, "What will it mean for *me* if I get involved with this person?" The Good Samaritan asked, "What will it mean for *this victim of violence* if I do *not* get involved in helping him?"

    d. Christians are to pattern their servant life on Jesus' servant life (John 13:34): "Love one another *as I have loved you.*"

4 Sin is the failure or refusal to serve God and others. By nature, people are turned in on themselves (Latin: *incurvatus in se*) and live to serve themselves (***figures in posture of indifference, symbols for sin***). They are controlled by "the lusts of the flesh," Romans 7:5.

Christians are to treat others as God has treated them. They are to be living images, living reflections, of God's character, Genesis 1:26,27; 1 Corinthians 10:31.

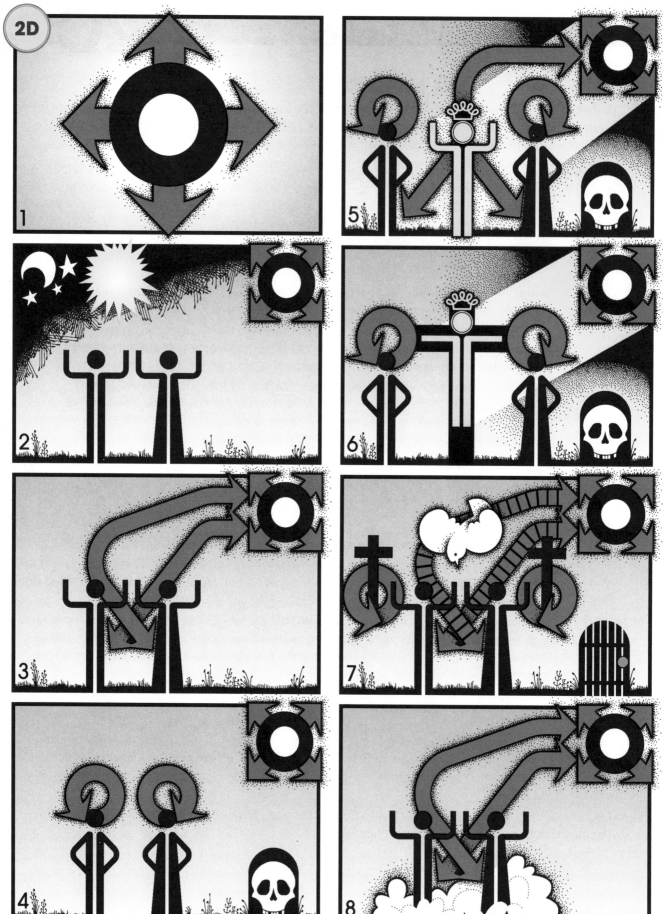

The numbers below relate to the numbered sections in **ILLUSTRATION 2D**.

1 "In the beginning, God…" Genesis 1:1 (*symbol for God*).

2 "created the heavens and the earth," Genesis 1:1 (*sun, moon, and stars*; *surface of earth*). "Then God said, 'Let us make humankind,'" Genesis 1:26. "Male and female He created them," Genesis 1:27 (*male and female figures*).

3 "in our image, after our likeness," Genesis 1:26 (*people serve God and one another with out-going love*).

4 Humanity sinned (*people live to serve themselves*; *note the break in the ground between the figures*). Death is the consequence (*tombstone with skull*), Romans 5:12, 6:23.

5 *People* changed. *God* did not. God became human in *Jesus*, and *lived for us the life we were meant to live*—but cannot.

6 *Jesus suffered the death we deserve to die.* He did it *for us*. We do not have to die as punishment for sin any more, Galatians 4:4,5.

7 Jesus lived a sinless life for us, died to suffer the punishment we deserve, and rose again from the grave as Lord over death and eternity. He is among us through His Holy Spirit (*dove*).

　　a. He assures us that our sins are forgiven (*cross through sin*).

　　b. Death is transformed into a doorway leading to God's Eternal Home (*door with slats*). We can "see" in faith what lies on the other side of death.

　　c. Now we are to live as God first intended us to live (*arrows to God and neighbor*). The lines forming the arrows are *broken*, because our obedience is, at best, imperfect.

8 In the life to come (the *cloud* symbolizes God's presence), God will restore things to the way He first intended them to be. In eternity, we shall perfectly *praise God and serve others*.

Love? What's That?

People today tend to confuse the biblical word *love* with the concept of *like*, or even "warmer" and "fuzzier" notions. However, God does not command us to *like* people, but to *love* and serve them. The English language uses the one word *love* to express several Greek words, four of which are depicted in **ILLUSTRATION 2E**.

 EROS (AIR-ose) is *attraction* to another, to benefit the self. It wishes to possess what it sees, and often results from sexual desire. It is a response of the emotions and cannot be commanded. (This word is not used in the New Testament.)

 PHILIA (FIL-ee-ah) refers to *friendship*, or *brotherly love*, such as the friendship Jonathan demonstrated toward David, 1 Samuel 18:1–4.

The Greeks also spoke of:

- *philadelphia*, "love of brother," and
- *philanthropia*, "love of humanity."

STORGE (STORE-gay) is affection in the rough-and-tumble give-and-take of *family life*. It is the love of parents for children, children for parents, and siblings for one another. It does not involve sexual feelings.

AGAPE (Ah-GAH-pay) acts in response to a *need* of another. It desires to benefit the other person. It is an act of the will and can be commanded. It is best translated as *service*. The Bible uses the word *agape* to speak of:

- God's love for humanity, and
- the love people are to have for one another.

Caring for Self to Use Life for Others

God made us. God owns us. God endows us with abilities. God wants us to care for and develop ourselves for use as God's instruments in the service of others.

ILLUSTRATION 2F depicts in yellow a ***person's face and upper body, with arms and fingers extended***. The person is shown within a ***circle divided into four segments*** representing people's volitional, emotional, physical, and intellectual powers. Under the ***symbol for God*** is a ***double-headed arrow*** denoting service to God and neighbor, and the ***symbol for sin***—with a ***question mark*** near each. The question mark asks, "Who is directing our walk through life? God (*left*), or the power of sin (*right*)?"

When Jesus engaged in a debate with a lawyer, the lawyer defined God's will for humanity as follows:

> *You shall love the Lord your God with all your* heart, *and with all your* soul, *and with all your* strength, *and with all your* mind; *and your neighbor as yourself.* (Luke 10:25–27)

Jesus not only *agreed* with him, but told him to *do* these things. The segments within the large circle contain symbols designed to help us understand the terms *heart, soul, strength,* and *mind*.

1 **Heart** (*upper left segment*)

The term "heart" refers to our volitional powers. "With all your heart" means "with all your will." God wants us to have an informed will (**law-codes**) equipped to weigh moral issues (**balance** or **scales**). As with a **traffic light**, God wants us to know when not to proceed (**red**), when to proceed with caution (**amber**), and when to proceed with a good conscience (**green**). God's will for us is that we learn to reflect Jesus' servant life in all that we do (**servant figure on law-codes**).

2 **Soul** (*upper right segment*)

God wants to empower us to develop a Christ-like *demeanor* that attracts others to us, equips us to serve them, and creates unity within our immediate and extended community. Our happy external demeanor (**smiling face-mask**) reflects our inner disposition and helps establish links between us and others; this makes them more willing to listen to any witness that we might wish to make to them. An unhappy external demeanor (**unhappy face-mask**) creates barriers between us and others. The **faces within the segment itself** reflect a variety of moods and dispositions.

3 **Strength** (*lower right segment*)

This segment contains symbols of **fruits**, **cake**, **candy**, **drink**, and a **person playing tennis**. God wants us to eat and drink healthfully, and to exercise to keep fit. Our bodies are then more likely to be instruments God can use to serve others (**servant figure**), rather than liabilities others must serve. God has also empowered people to provide health care to those needing it (**serpent around staff**, Numbers 21:4–9).

4 **Mind** (*lower left segment*)

God wants us to study things that will edify and equip us to serve others better (**graduation hat**, **diplomas**, **books**).

God writes the agenda for our actions. We serve others as *God* wants us to serve them—not as *we* might want to serve them, or as *they* might want to be served. "You shall love your neighbor as yourself" does not mean "50% for others and 50% for me." God wants us to devote life 100% to serving God by serving others.

Our goal is to become more what God intends us to be, so that we might in turn help others become what God intends them to be.

ILLUSTRATION 2G portrays some of the thoughts that go through people's minds as they contemplate doing Bible study—or as they actually do it.

1 Some do it merely to collect a **diploma** or a **certificate**, or perhaps to please someone else.

2 Some undertake Bible study to equip themselves to win arguments about religion. They plan to use the Bible to bash others (*note the **victim** in the lower left corner*).

3 Many people are afraid of taking a Bible into *their **hands***. They fear that it might get *its* hands on *them*! They are partly right—for indeed, through the Bible, God seeks to draw people to Himself in the "embrace of grace" (***hands on woman's shoulders***).

4 Some have the mistaken notion that the Bible contains nothing but commandments they must try to keep if they are to make it to and through the "pearly gates" into heaven—into God's eternal presence (***cloud***). Often they are not sure (***question mark***) they want to be all that good (***halo***).

5 When we spend time reading the Bible, we find that it offers us a message that is all joy and good news (***happy face***).

6 The Bible offers each of us personally a grand gift—the forgiveness of sins through Jesus' ***cross***, and membership in God's community of saints (***halo***).

7 When God brings us to faith in Jesus the Messiah, God does not call us to ***rest on His Word*** (*as on a mattress*), but to that true rest, which is life in fellowship with Jesus, Matthew 11:28–30. The person depicted is confusing Christian *vocation* with Christian *vacation*.

8 Jesus calls His followers to serve one another—even as Jesus served His disciples, John 13:1–15 (***person washing another person's feet***).

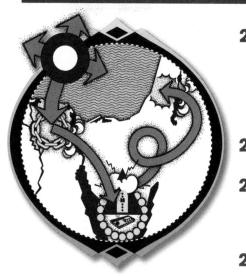

2A The Bible is more than a book. It is a library of books—referred to as the Old and New Testaments. The Protestant Old Testament books consist of the writings found in the Jewish Scriptures. Roman Catholic and Orthodox Churches include additional (Apocryphal) books in the Old Testament section of their Bible.

2B People hold a variety of opinions concerning the nature of God.

2C The Bible says that God's character is best summed up by the word "love," and that God desires people to show their love for God by loving and serving others.

2D When God first created the universe and humanity, He had a specific plan in mind. Although humanity sinned, God acted through Jesus the Messiah to gather people of all nations into fellowship with Himself in forgiving grace, and to empower fallen humanity to know and fulfill His original plan.

2E The English language ascribes to the word "love" a variety of meanings. However, when the Bible commands people to love God and others, the word *love* is best understood as *serve*.

2F God's desire is that we develop our volitional, emotional, physical, and intellectual powers as much as possible to serve others to the best of our ability, and to help others in turn become more of what God intended them to be: people who dedicate life to glorifying God by serving others.

2G Although people undertake Bible study for a variety of reasons, God's desire is to draw us into fellowship with Himself in forgiving grace, and to teach and empower us to serve one another in community.

CROSS WAYS®

1
SECTION

UNITS 1–10

From Creation
to the Transjordan

UNIT 3
In the Beginning

God's Purposes in Creation and History

NASA photo

ILLUSTRATION 3A depicts *Planet Earth*—the "home" God has provided for humanity. No borders, flags, or skin colors would be visible unless you had a very powerful lens. The ways in which we subdivide the human family is not in keeping with God's will.

Statements by two U.S. astronauts help us see our home from outer space.

James Irwin, who walked the moon during the 1971 Apollo 15 mission, wrote:

> *The Earth reminded us of a Christmas tree ornament hanging in the blackness of space. As we got farther and farther away it diminished in size. Finally it shrank to the size of a marble, the most beautiful marble you can imagine. That beautiful, warm, living object looked so fragile, so delicate, that if you touched it with a finger it would crumble and fall apart. Seeing this has to change a person, has to make a person appreciate the creation of God and the love of God.*

While on board the *Discovery* Space Shuttle on November 1, 1998, John Glenn said:

> *I don't think you can be up here and look out the window as I did the first day and see Earth from this vantage point, to look out at this kind of creation and not believe in God. To me, it's impossible—it just strengthens my faith. I wish there were words to describe what it's like… truly awesome.*

3B

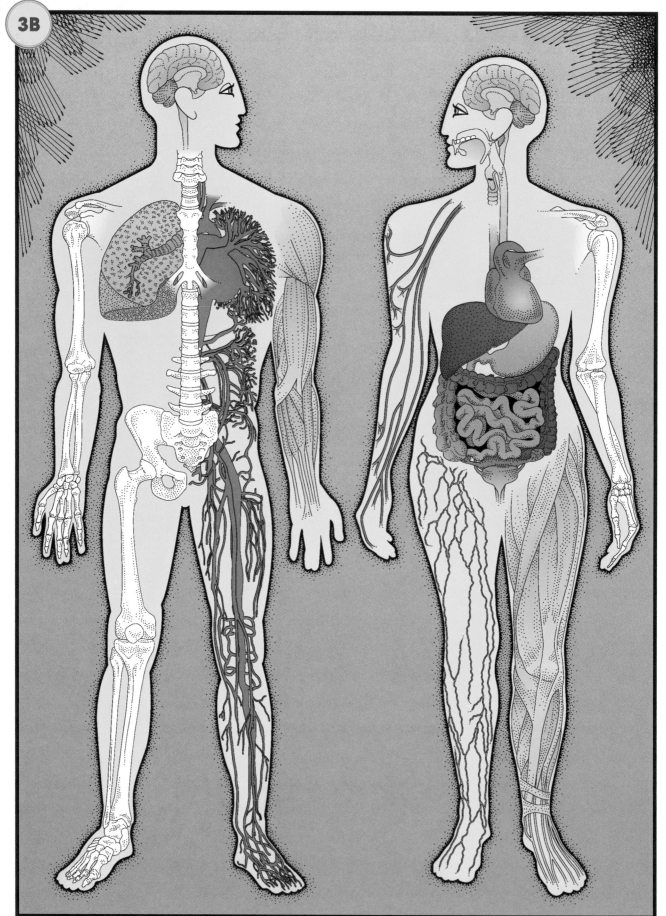

The Wonder That We Are

ILLUSTRATION 1A and **ILLUSTRATION 1B** remind us that when we look at the heavens through a telescope, we see a vast universe. **ILLUSTRATION 3B**, which depicts a male and a female body, helps us understand that when we study the human body through a microscope, we see another incredible universe.

1 If we could join end-to-end all the ***veins, arteries, and capillaries*** found in the average human body, they would reach from 2½ to 4 times around the equator—or 60,000 to 100,000 miles (97,000 to 160,000 kilometers).

2 It we could flatten out the components that make up the ***large and small intestines***, they would cover three football or soccer fields.

3 The ***brain*** is made up of about 10 billion nerve cells or neurons. Each cell is like a tiny octopus, with many connection points on each of its many "arms." One researcher, Professor Pyotr Anokhin, a disciple of Pavlov in the field of psychology, estimated the number of connections and pathways that could be made by a normal brain: the number 1 followed by 6.25 million miles (10 million kilometers) of zeros. If one could unravel all the tiny fibers that make up the average human brain, they would stretch approximately to the moon and back.

4 The body houses the most amazing pumping device in the world—the human ***heart***. Its record of work is about 72 pumping actions per minute, 100,000 per day, 35 million per year, and 2.5 billion in the average lifetime. It manages to do this, even though it produces only about $\frac{1}{240}$ of a horsepower for the job. Each beat musters enough energy to lift a two-pound weight (0.9 kilogram) one foot (30 centimeters). Each day the heart generates enough energy to lift a man 500 feet (152 meters). Blood passes through the body at about six inches (15 centimeters) per second. It takes about 18 seconds for blood to travel from the heart to the foot and back again, and about eight seconds for the journey to and from the brain.

5 The human ***eye*** has about 130 million light receptors and about 7 million sensory terminals for sight. Each eye has about 300,000 "lines" going to the brain. These break down the scene observed and re-arrange it within the brain to create the sense of vision. Although the eye transmits pictures to the brain upside-down, the brain sees them right-side up.

6 The human ***ear*** is the most amazing acoustical instrument in the world. When we strike a chord on the piano, we think the piano makes a sound. It does not—it merely makes vibrations in the air. The human ear picks these up and interprets them as sound. When we strike two notes next to each other on the piano, the difference in the pitch is obvious. However, the human ear can hear 15 distinct pitches between the two notes. Although a pianist usually has 88 notes to choose from, the human ear can discern about 15,000.

The inner ear of an adult is no larger than it was on the day of birth. Its size never changes. It has to be this way. If it did alter, there would be a variation in sound perceived throughout the growing years of life—from a high-pitched impression in infancy to a low-pitched impression in adulthood. God knew that would lead to confusion, and so made the inner ear as it is.

In Psalm 139:13,14, we read:

> *It was You who formed my inward parts;*
> *You knit me together in my mother's womb.*
> *I praise You, for I am fearfully and wonderfully made.*

God, Creator and Owner

ILLUSTRATION 3C shows *Planet Earth* and a *human being*, with *God's ownership label* attached to each.

Upper section

  God made and owns the universe, including Planet Earth. Everything belongs to God. We humans create and own nothing. We merely use what belongs to God, and are to do so responsibly.

  In the parable of the rich fool (Luke 12:13–21), Jesus reminded His audience that it was the *land*, not the *man*, that produced abundantly—and *God owns the land*.

Lower section

  God made and owns *all people* on Planet Earth. Again in Luke 12:13–21, Jesus reminded the rich fool that *his very life was being lent to him by God*, and that very night *God would demand that the rich man's life-on-loan be returned to its Owner. The rich man was about to die.*

② God has endowed us with faculties and abilities. We are to view these with respect, develop them responsibly and wisely, and use them to glorify God by serving others.

③ Our actions toward others are to reflect God's prior actions toward us, 1 John 4:19–21. We do not love others so that God may love us; we love others to reflect the wonderful truth that God already loves us.

④ When we live according to God's will reflected in the life of Jesus the Messiah, we find meaning and joy in life, and we bring meaning and joy to others.

Those who confess the Apostle's Creed declare, "I believe in God the Father Almighty, Maker of Heaven and Earth." The biblical truth concerning God's relationship with creation might be expressed better if two words were added to this first section of the Apostles' Creed: "I believe in God the Father Almighty, Maker *and Owner* of Heaven and Earth."

Although people like to speak of "their" country, house, car, money, body, etc., the biblical truth is that God made and owns all things. **People are merely entrusted with the management of God's property.**

Therefore instead of talking about "Christian giving," we should talk about "Christian management" and "Christian distribution." We humans merely handle and use that which belongs to God. We have no right to use the personal pronoun "my" in relation to the ownership of anything.

The Original Plan

1   **ILLUSTRATION 3D** depicts God's original plan for humanity. God's plan was that all people would live together:

- under God as King (***crown***, and the ***symbol for God***);
- as one united family (***community of people holding hands around Planet Earth***);
- with each person asking, "How can I use life to glorify God by serving those around me?" (***servant figures***, ***arrows from each to God and neighbor***, ***law-codes***).

2   God's plan was that there would be unity and harmony:

- among all people;
- between the sexes (***man and woman serving God and each other*** (upper section), and ***holding hands*** (bottom border; man has ***yellow buttons on jacket sleeve***, woman has ***pink nails***);
- among everyone in different positions and situations in society.

3   God says to each of us:

> Seek under My grace and power
> > to become more and more what I want you to be,
>
> so that I can use you more effectively
> > to help others become more and more
> > > what I want them to be.

4   In today's fallen and sinful world, we are to serve others as God wants us to serve them—not as they might want us to serve them, nor as we might want to serve them. God writes the agenda. Each of us is to become more Christ-like, and to help others become more Christ-like.

5   Unity would prevail at all levels if every person on the face of Planet Earth asked only:

> "How can I use life to glorify God by serving others?"

6   In Ephesians 1:9,10, St. Paul defines the mission of God's people as follows:

> *God has made known to us in all wisdom and insight the mystery of His will, which He set forth in Christ as a plan for the fullness of time, to unite all things in Him, things in heaven and things on earth.* (RSV translation)

Genesis 1:1–2:4a

Still today, some Christian communities set out their statements of faith under *We Believe* and *We Reject*. Similarly, in Genesis 1:1–2:4a, the writer sets forth positive statements about the true God, and rejects prevailing false beliefs. The passage makes the following points—explicitly and implicitly:

1
We believe: **There is only one God.**
We reject: There are many gods.

2
We believe: **God is asexual. Although the Bible speaks of God as "He," it does not ascribe "male-ness" or "female-ness" to God.**
We reject: There are male and female deities. (The Hebrew language does not have a word for goddess.)

3
We believe: **God created everything through His all-powerful Word.**
We reject: God used preexisting materials to form the universe.

4
We believe: **The sun, moon, and stars are lamps God has set in place to provide light and divide time.**
We reject: The heavenly bodies are deities people must worship. (See Deuteronomy 4:15–19.)

5
We believe: **History had a beginning, and has a purpose and a goal.**
We reject: Humanity is locked into a closed, repetitious cycle of history that goes nowhere.

6
We believe: **The creation of humanity was the grand finale of the creative process.**
We reject: Humanity was an afterthought in the creative process.

7
We believe: **Humanity was made to live in an "I—Thou" relationship with God, and to manage the created order for God responsibly.**
We reject: Humanity was made to do the gods' "dirty work" on earth.

8
We believe: **The created order brings forth its fruits in response to God's controlling hand and word of command.** (See Genesis 1:11–12.)
We reject: People can manipulate the gods to provide bountifully for humanity's needs by performing rites and rituals involving sexual acts.

9
We believe: **God's purposes in creation were good, and the created order is inherently good.**
We reject: God is in some way responsible for the evil that exists in creation.

10
We believe: **Creation came into existence in an orderly fashion; God is a God of order.**
We reject: Creation came into existence as the result of an initial chaotic struggle among the gods.

11
We believe: **Order continues in creation because of God's command and rule.**
We reject: Continuing order in creation depends upon the rituals people perform.

12
We believe: **It is important for humanity to render due praise and worship to God, especially on the Sabbath. If God saw fit to rest on the Sabbath, it is important for humanity to follow God's example.**
We reject: Whether, when, or how one worships God is merely a matter of whim.

Literary Patterns

Genesis 1:1–2:4a

1 Numerous literary patterns can be detected in Genesis 1:1–2:4a. There is an obvious link between *Day One* and *Day Four*, between *Day Two* and *Day Five*, and between *Day Three* and *Day Six*.

> *Day One*…God begins His creative activity, and day and night appear.
> *Day Four*…God creates the heavenly lights—the stars and the planets.
>
> *Day Two*…God creates the sky and sea.
> *Day Five*…God places birds in the sky, and fish in the sea.
>
> *Day Three*…God creates the land and plants.
> *Day Six*…God creates land animals and humans.
>
> *Day Seven*…God rests.

- The first three days describe a process of *separation*.
- The second three days focus on *population*.
- The final day speaks of *celebration*.

2 There are more complicated patterns. There are seven parts in the events of the various days of creation (one or two of the parts are missing from some of the days):

    a.   "And God said"

    b.   "Let there be"

    c.   "And it was so"

    d.   The particulars are restated.

    e.   A name is given, or blessings conferred.

    f.   "And God saw that it was good"

    g.   "And there was evening and there was morning"

Where some of the parts are omitted, other details are added to create a balance in the events of each day. For example, God's works are doubled on the third and sixth days.

3 Other literary frameworks can be detected. The presence of these patterns indicates that Genesis 1:1–2:4a is a special kind of writing. The numerous literary patterns within it point to a form of writing intended to aid memory. The use of memory, and oral tradition, played a much bigger role in the ancient world than it does in today's world, since important events were preserved in this way before alphabets and writing were developed.

4 Although Genesis 1 contains magnificent truths about creation's origin and order, it is not an eye-witness report of days one through seven of human history. The passage is strongly liturgical in tone and, very likely, was used in worship rituals. To read Genesis 1 without feeling moved to praise God is to miss the point of the chapter.

Two Creation Accounts

Some refer to Genesis 1:1–2:4a as *Creation Account 1* and to Genesis 2:4b–25 as *Creation Account 2*. This gives rise to discussion about how they agree and differ.

Genesis 1:1–2:4a

Although Genesis 1:1–2:4a speaks about the creation *process*, it looks beyond God's creative *actions* to stress that God made everything *good*—and states this seven times. The following points surface in this passage—explicitly and implicitly.

 God *created* the universe and all that is in it.

 God is a God of *order.* God created the universe to function in an orderly manner, materially and morally.

 God created everything *good.* God cannot be blamed for the existence of chaos in the realms of nature and morality.

 The *false views* of surrounding nations about the origin of the universe are to be rejected.

5 Genesis 1 presents a high *anthropology*, declaring the creation of humanity to have been the climax of the creative process.

6 Genesis 1 gives *meaning* to history. It declares that there was a "beginning," indicating that history has a purpose and an ultimate end.

7 People are given an exalted *purpose and mission*—to demonstrate God's character and likeness. Because people are to be God's walking and living images, God is opposed to images made of wood and stone.

8 God *made*, and *still owns*, all things. Humanity was not given *ownership* of anything, but was entrusted with the *responsible use* of everything.

9 God cannot be manipulated. Nature produces its bounty in response to God's command to produce—not in response to any rituals that people perform. "Daily bread" is, in the final analysis, a gift of God, despite any human sweat that might go into its production. We cannot *manipulate* God—we can only *submit* to God.

10 Humanity's awareness of God's power, ownership, control, wisdom, and goodness in creation is to move people to *praise and worship* God—particularly on the Sabbath.

Genesis 2:4b–25

Genesis 2:4b–25 has a much less theological tone to it than Genesis 1:1–2:4a.

 God does not create from a distance through God's all-powerful word, but engages in creative activity on the face of the earth itself. The face of the earth seems to be rather bare.

 God fashions man from the dust of the earth, as a potter molding clay. Indeed, God makes man from the dust of the ground to which man must eventually return if man sins, Genesis 3:19. God fashions man, and then breathes into his nostrils the breath of life. Note the close relationship between Creator and creature, and how dependent man is on God for life.

 After forming man, God plants a garden in which are two mysterious trees. Man is to care for the garden and may eat of all its trees except "the tree of the knowledge of good and evil," Genesis 2:17.

4 God then declares that it is not good for man to be alone, and provides him with a companion. In doing this, God first makes animals and birds, and brings them to man for naming—but no suitable companion for man is found among them.

5 Finally, God makes a woman out of man's flesh and bone, and brings her to him. Man is thrilled, and exclaims "this at last." Man's companion has not been made from the dust as were the animals and birds, but from his own bone and flesh. The relationship between man and woman supersedes all others. They become one, and sense no shame in their nakedness.

THE RELATIONSHIP BETWEEN THE TWO CREATION ACCOUNTS

1 It seems inadequate to understand Genesis 2 as merely a creation account, or as an alternate or additional creation account to supplement Genesis 1. In style, language, and content, Genesis 2:4b–25 belongs to a much larger section, Genesis 2:4b–11:9, which answers the question that flows out of Genesis 1: "If God made all things, if God arranged them all in an orderly manner, if God made all things good, if God intended humanity to enjoy God's good creation forever, what went wrong?" Genesis 2–11 answers those questions.

2 When chapter and verse divisions were introduced into the Bible by the French printer, Stephanus, in the 16th century, Genesis 2–3 was divided into two chapters, giving the impression that it is two different episodes. It is not. It is a single narrative in which the divine drama gets under way. Genesis 2–3 is a narrative in which the stage curtains are pulled back, the setting is described, and the first two human characters in the divine drama are introduced. However, these humans bring sin, chaos, and death into God's good, beneficent, and orderly world.

3 While Genesis 1 states that God acted only in goodness, wisdom, love and providence, Genesis 2–3 (and more broadly Genesis 2–11) state that humanity responded with rebellion and ingratitude.

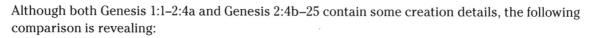

Although both Genesis 1:1–2:4a and Genesis 2:4b–25 contain some creation details, the following comparison is revealing:

	Genesis 1:1–2:4a	Genesis 2:4b–25
1	Reads like a hymn, a confession of faith. Liturgical in tone.	A story with characters, action, and a plot.
2	Careful arrangement of materials. Repetition of phrases. Distinct vocabulary.	No orderly arrangement. No repetition of words or phrases. Distinct vocabulary.
3	Man and woman created last, after trees and animal life.	Man is made first, then trees, animals, and, finally, woman.
4	Concerns itself with the universe.	Concerns itself only with the earth, as directly related to humankind's existence.
5	God creates from a distance, using words.	God's creative action is spoken of in human terms. God molds like a potter, and walks in the garden in the cool of the day.
6	Male and female are created.	Man is formed from the ground, and woman is formed from the rib of man.
7	The beginning state of things is chaotic and watery.	The beginning state of things is desert-like, with water viewed as life-giving.

Both passages contain common emphases:

Genesis 1:1–2:4a	Genesis 2:4b–25
1 Both passages ascribe creation to the *free and spontaneous initiative of God*, whose disposition is love, goodness, and providence.	
2 God brought creation into existence in *perfect and effortless freedom*.	
3 The created order is good.	
4 Humanity is the *high point* of the creative process, created to live in the closest fellowship with God.	
5 People are *social beings*; it is not good for people to be alone.	
6 Creation is to serve humanity's needs. At the same time, humanity is to use and care for God's property responsibly.	

3A We mere mortals live on a tiny planet adorned and decorated with God's handiwork.

3B When we look at the heavens through a telescope, we see a wondrous universe. When we study the human body through a microscope, we see another amazing universe.

3C God made and owns the universe, and God made and owns all people on Planet Earth. We humans do not own anything; we simply use and manage what belongs to God.

3D When God created the first humans, His plan was that they and their descendants should live together in caring community, seeking to glorify God and to serve each other in their thoughts, words, and deeds.

3E Genesis 1:1–2:4a is a highly structured creation account. It focuses on:
- The *Who* and *why* of creation, rather than on the *when* and the *how*;
- What truths God's people are to *believe*, and what falsehoods they are to *reject*.

3F Numerous literary patterns are woven into Genesis 1:1–2:4a. The overall purpose is to summon humanity to praise the God who made and owns all things. Despite the complexity of the structure of Genesis 1:1–2:4a, it contains obvious emphases:
- God made all things *good*.
- God made creation in an orderly manner, and designed it to function that way.

3G The structure of Genesis 2:4b–25 is less complex.
- It makes no reference to a seven-day creation process, and speaks of God forming the created order and humanity in the manner of a potter molding clay.
- It is closely linked to chapter 3—a narrative that answers the question, "If God made all things *good*, what went *wrong*?"

3H Although the contents of Genesis 1:1–2:4a and Genesis 2:4b–25 might be understood in terms of looking at the origin of creation and humanity through two different lenses, both passages contain similar emphases. Both set the stage for the huge narrative that follows.

CROSS WAYS®

1 SECTION

UNITS 1–10

From Creation to the Transjordan

UNIT 4
The Biblical Overture

The Effects of Sin and God's Response

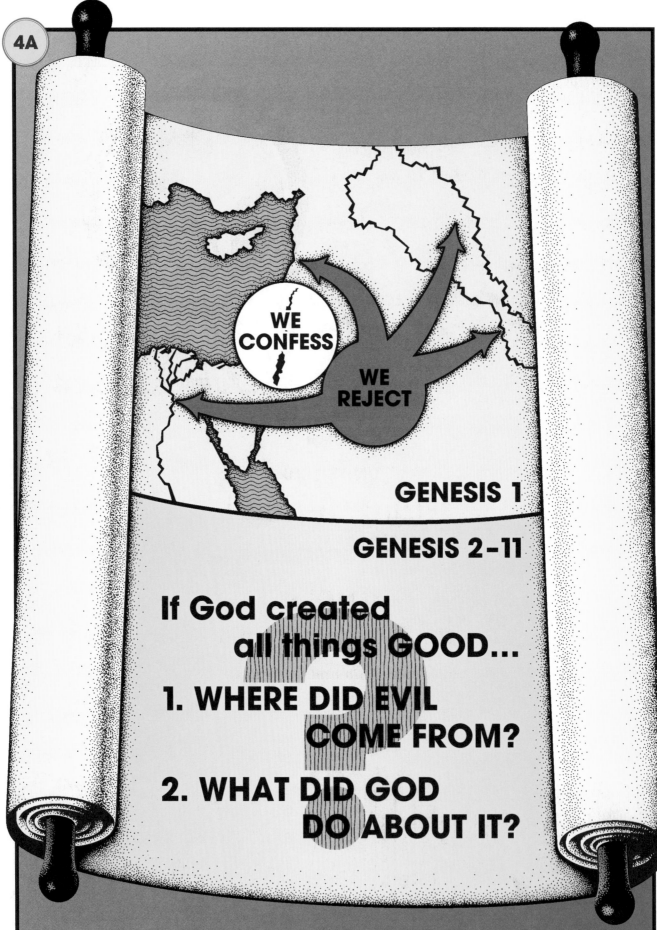

The following activity helps explain the role of Genesis 1–11 in relation to the rest of the Bible.

- *First*, note that Abraham is mentioned for the first time in the Bible in Genesis 11:26.
- *Second*, place between the fingers of your left hand those pages of the Bible which outline what happened before Abraham appeared on the stage of history—that's Genesis 1:1–11:25.
- *Third*, hold between the fingers of your right hand the pages of the Bible which report what happened beyond the call of Abraham—that's the rest of the Old Testament and all of the New Testament. You will have about ten pages in your left hand and a thousand in your right.

The point of the activity? The Bible devotes only one percent of its pages to what happened *before* Abraham's call, and ninety-nine percent of its pages to events *after* his call. What role, then, does Genesis 1–11 play in the larger biblical narrative?

When a musical show is performed in a theater, the orchestra often plays an overture before the curtain rises. The overture gives the audience a taste of what is to come. Genesis 1–11 performs this role in the biblical narrative. These chapters introduce God, His plans for creation and humanity, and the spirit in which He deals with humanity's rebellion against Him.

ILLUSTRATION 4A depicts the central themes that emerge in the biblical overture.

Upper section

Genesis 1:1–2:4a sets forth Israel's beliefs concerning the origin and purpose of the created order, and rejects the views of surrounding nations.

 The illustration shows a ***circle over the land of Israel***, in which are the words, **WE CONFESS**. God's Old Testament people embraced specific truths about the God of creation and the purpose of creation and history.

 In a ***second circle*** are the words, **WE REJECT**. Arrows protrude from it to surrounding nations. God's Old Testament people rejected the beliefs of neighboring nations concerning divine beings and the purpose of life.

Lower section

The insistence of Genesis 1:1–2:4a that ***God created all things*** and that He made them ***GOOD*** raises two key questions:

 WHERE DID EVIL COME FROM?

WHAT DID GOD DO ABOUT IT?

Genesis 2:4b–11:32, and the rest of the Bible, grapple with these questions.

4B

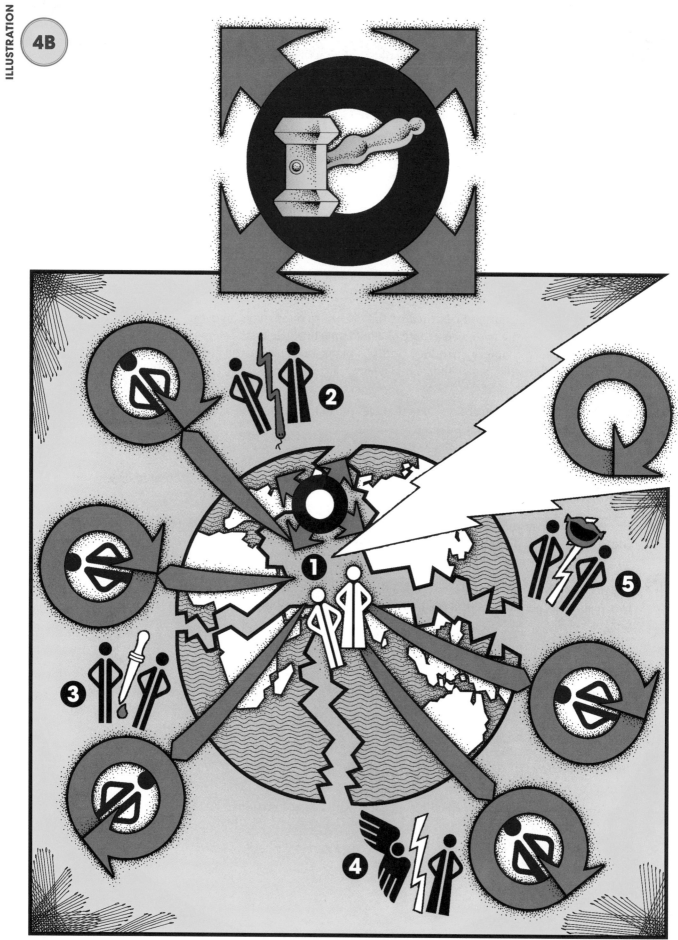

The Entry of Sin

ILLUSTRATION 3D depicts the order and wisdom of God's original plan. People were to live in harmony and unity.

ILLUSTRATION 4B shows the devastating power of sin (*symbol for sin*, *center right*) breaking in and destroying God's original plan.

Sin makes people prisoners to self—prisoners to their own whims and will (*persons locked inside symbols for sin*). The spirit of community is gone. The curse of individualism prevails.

Sin tore apart God's good creation at all levels. It shattered the relationship between:

❶ **God and humanity** (*symbol for God*, *male and female figures*);

❷ **man and woman**, **male and female**, Genesis 2,3 (*male and female figures*, *dividing serpent*);

❸ **brother and brother**, Genesis 4. Cain killed Abel (*two figures*, *knife*, *drop of blood*);

❹ **the heavenly and the earthly**, Genesis 6:1–4. Divine beings called the "sons of God" were sexually intimate with women on earth (*winged creature*; *female figure*, Job 1:6, 2:1; 38:7);

❺ **nation and nation**, Genesis 11:1–9. The building of the tower of Babel resulted in the confusion of languages, the fragmenting of humanity (*two figures*, *mouth*), and the scattering of language groups across the world.

God declares the human race to be under judgment (*gavel on symbol for God*). People first made from dust must return to dust, Genesis 3:19. They must die.

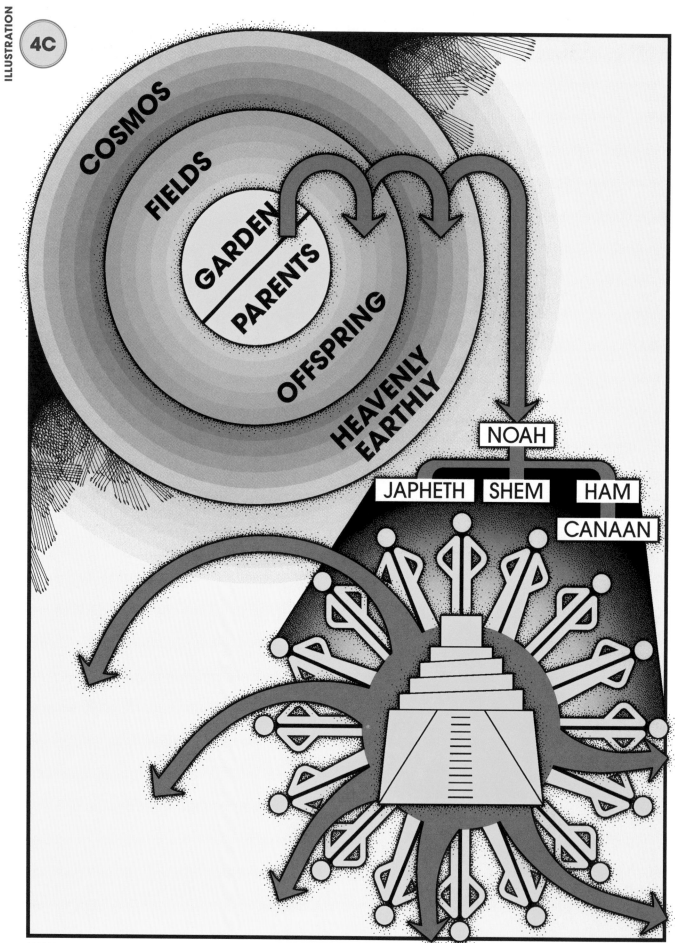

The Spread of Sin

When a pebble is thrown into a pool, there is a ripple effect; waves spread across the pool's surface. **ILLUSTRATION 4C**, based on Genesis 2–11, depicts how, after the power of sin broke into history, sin's ripple effect spread across God's good creation.

Upper left section

1 Genesis 2–3 forms a single narrative. In Genesis 2, history's stage and scenery are set in place (**GARDEN** of Eden), and humanity's **PARENTS** (Adam and Eve) are introduced in preparation for the events described in Genesis 3.

In Genesis 3, the serpent tempts Eve to sin. Eve in turn tempts Adam, and he succumbs. In striving to be free from God's control, Adam and Eve become slaves to self, to human desires, and to the lusts of the flesh.

After sinning, they try to hide from God and cover themselves with loincloths made of *fig leaves*. God looks for them, confronts them, spells out the consequences of their actions, and covers them with *skins*, Genesis 3:8–21. **God deals with sinful humanity in loving, forgiving grace.**

2 In Genesis 4, the cycle of sin, human reaction, and sin's effects are repeated. While Cain and Abel are working out in the **FIELDS**, Cain kills his brother Abel—"like parents, like offspring." The power and effects of sin spread from the *GARDEN* to the *FIELDS* and from *PARENTS* to **OFFSPRING**.

3 The power of sin now spreads across all creation—across the **COSMOS**. Genesis 6:1–4 refers to "the sons of God" (Job 1:6, 2:1, 38:7) being sexually intimate with earthly women. The term *sons of God* in Genesis 6:1–4 is interpreted in several ways: as angels, as the righteous descendants of Adam's son, Seth (Genesis 4:25,26), or (most probably) as divine beings. The message seems to be: There is now an inappropriate overlap between **HEAVENLY** and **EARTHLY** beings. God now declares the human family to be totally corrupt, Genesis 6:5.

Lower right section

1 God pushed back the waters to expose the land mass when He first created the world, Genesis 1:9,10. God now summons the waters back to destroy the first creation, 7:11. Later, God pushes the waters back to make a new beginning to creation, 8:13,14. **NOAH** and his three sons (**JAPHETH**, **SHEM**, and **HAM**) and their respective wives survive the flood, and through them God makes a new beginning to the history of humanity, chs. 9, 10.

Later, when Ham sees Noah drunk and naked, he tells his two brothers what he has seen. Japheth and Shem cover their father. When Noah recovers from his drunken state, he places a curse on Ham's son, **CANAAN** (9:18–25), but blesses Shem and Japheth, 9:26,27. (After the Israelites entered the Promised Land under Joshua, they set about destroying the Canaanites, whom they considered to be cursed by God.)

2 ***The Tower of Babel:*** People fear that they will be scattered. So, "to make a name for themselves," they begin to build a tower that will reach up into the heavens. God stops the project by confusing the people's speech and scattering humanity (***arrows protruding from tower***) across the face of the earth, 11:1–9.

Sin has fragmented and scattered humanity. Its footprints now appear across all of creation.

From Adam to Abraham

The Bible refers to Abraham for the first time in Genesis 11:26; he is the first of the so-called "Chosen People." The first eleven chapters of the Bible outline what happened *before* Abraham's call. The rest of the Bible's contents describes what happened *after* his call. Genesis 1–11 defines *God's purpose* in calling Abraham and in forming from him a people eventually referred to as the Israelites, Genesis 32:28.

SIN-JUDGMENT-GRACE

Genesis 1 declares that God (*symbol for God*), who is *GOOD*, made a *good creation* (**ILLUSTRATION 4D**, *top segment*). The first parents were to praise and serve God, and serve each other. Key themes run through the four major narratives that follow in Genesis 2–11, with God's *GRACE* (God's *undeserved mercy*) being the most important theme throughout.

1 Genesis 2–3
- **SIN:** Adam and Eve disobey God (*male and female figures, dividing serpent*).
- **JUDGMENT:** Their sin brings *DEATH* (*gavel* symbolizing judgment; *tombstone with skull*).
- **GRACE:** God remains in fellowship with them and *clothes them with skins*, 3:21.

2 Genesis 4–5
- **SIN:** Cain kills his brother Abel (*two figures, knife, drop of blood*).
- **JUDGMENT:** God banishes Cain from His presence (*pointing hand across Cain*—"*Depart*").
- **GRACE:** The Lord puts a protective mark on Cain, 4:15 (*mark; circle around Cain*).

3 Genesis 6–9
- **SIN:** Divine beings called "the sons of God" (Genesis 6:1–4; see Job 1:6, 2:1, 38:7) are sexually intimate with earthly women (*winged creature, female figure*).
- **JUDGMENT:** God destroys the face of Planet Earth with a *FLOOD* (*cloud, rain, waves*).
- **GRACE:** God preserves *NOAH*, his immediate family, and the animal world (*ark*).

4 Genesis 10:1–12:3
- **SIN:** Noah's descendants begin to build a *tower* to reach into the heavens "to make a name for themselves" and to prevent being scattered across the face of the earth.
- **JUDGMENT:** God stops the project by confusing their languages (*mouth*) and scattering the people.
- **GRACE:** God calls *ABRAHAM*, sends him to the *land of Canaan*, promises him *many descendants*, and declares that blessings (*cup*) will flow from them to the nations (*world*).

The Theology of Genesis 1–11

- Genesis 1–11 tells *who* created the universe, *why* God created it, *how humanity responded* to God's goodness, and *how God responded and responds* to people's sin and rebellion.
- Genesis 1–11 culminates in the call of *ABRAHAM*, 12:1–3. The God who calls Abraham is none other than the Creator. God is not acting in some new way, but, as always, in *GRACE*.
- God had a purpose in calling Abraham: **To work through Abraham and his descendants to restore humanity to God's original plan.** (Compare **ILLUSTRATION 3D** with **ILLUSTRATION 4B**.)

The *key word* that weaves its way through the biblical narrative from beginning to end is *GRACE!*

4A The narratives in Genesis 1,2 describe God's actions in creating the universe and humanity, and emphasize the fact that He made them "good." They reject the faith systems of other nations.

4B Genesis 3–11 deals with questions such as:

- What went wrong?
- Who is to blame?
- What effect did human sin have on creation and humanity?
- What did God do about it?

4C The narratives in Genesis 3–11 describe the ripple effect of sin.

- Sin spreads from parents to offspring, and from the garden to the fields.
- There is overlap between heavenly and earthly beings.
- The nations succumb to the power of sin.

4D Similar threads run through the four narratives in Genesis 3–11.

- Humanity acts consistently—*it sins*.
- God acts consistently. Initially, He declares humanity to be under *judgment*.
- However, God's *grace* prevails. He undertakes to draw fallen humanity back into fellowship with Himself and each other.

The overarching purpose of Genesis 1–11 is to set the stage for human history, and to explain why God called Abraham: to be the first of a people through whom God would work to restore creation and humanity to His original plan.

CROSS WAYS®

1 SECTION

UNITS 1–10

From Creation to the Transjordan

UNIT 5

A People—A Mission

The Origin and Mission of God's Chosen People

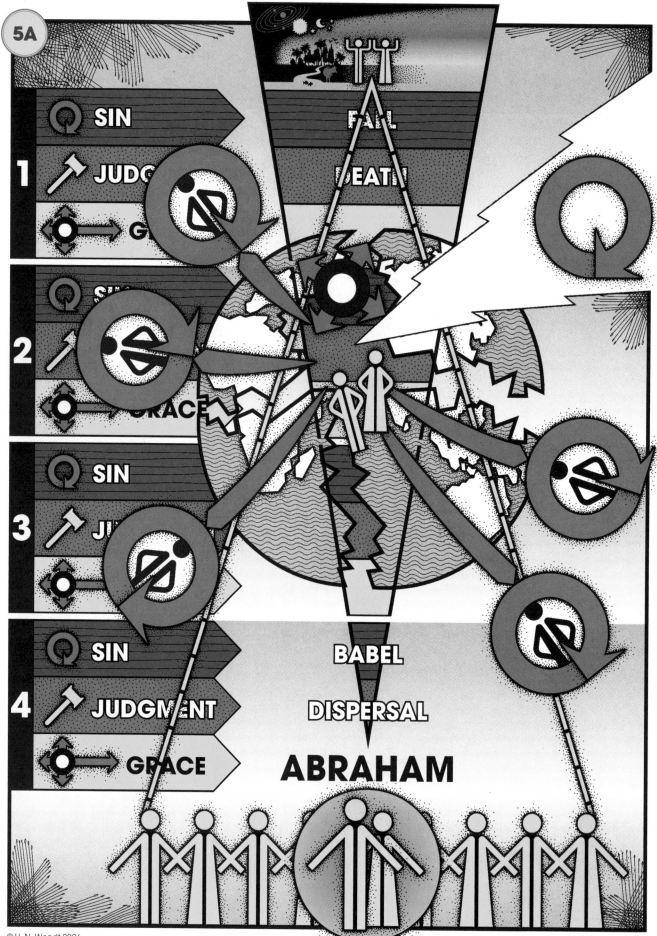

SIN

1 JUDG

G

SIN

2

GRACE

SIN

3 J

SIN

4 JUDGMENT

GRACE

FALL

DEATH

BABEL

DISPERSAL

ABRAHAM

How would you feel if the leader of your country were to tell you that you had been chosen for a very special task *within your country*? Overwhelmed! One day, a long time ago, God—the creator of the universe and the Lord of time and eternity—told Abraham that He had chosen him to serve as His instrument to launch a mission *to the world*. No doubt, Abraham was overwhelmed by the honor God's call bestowed on him.

ILLUSTRATION 5A depicts what took place. It combines **ILLUSTRATION 4B** and **ILLUSTRATION 4D**, and adds information of its own.

1 *Yellow dashed lines* spread out from beneath the *top-center segment* depicting **creation**, and descend to the outer limits of the **ten figures** at the *base of the illustration*. These lines remind us that, with the passing of time, the human race grew. (Obviously, there were more than ten people on Planet Earth when God called Abraham.)

2 Other descending **black lines**, that begin on either side of the *top-center segment* depicting **creation**, point to the persons in the center of the group of people, **ABRAHAM and Sarah**. The message is that God chose Abraham and Sarah to be the first of a special *mission people*.

3 What was God's purpose in choosing Abraham and Sarah? They were to be the first of a people through whom God planned to work—to reconcile humanity to Himself and one another. The details above Abraham and Sarah depict the **fragmented world** that sin caused. People no longer live to serve *God and others*; they live to serve *themselves*. *Community* gives way to *individualism*.

4 Why did God choose **ABRAHAM**?
   a. Although God's call was an honor for Abraham and his descendants, it nevertheless summoned them to a mission. That mission was, through God's forgiving and empowering grace, to draw humanity back into fellowship with God and each other.
   b. God did not choose Abraham because He believed that Abraham was more righteous than others, deserved God's call, or had great faith or leadership potential. When God called Abraham, he, like all his contemporaries, was an idolater, Joshua 24:2 (see **ILLUSTRATION 5C**, *idols*).
   c. One thing prompted God to call Abraham: **GRACE**—undeserved love and mercy! Grace has always been at the heart of God's dealings with humanity in general, and God's people in particular. It will remain so until the end of time.

5B

GENESIS ORIGINS

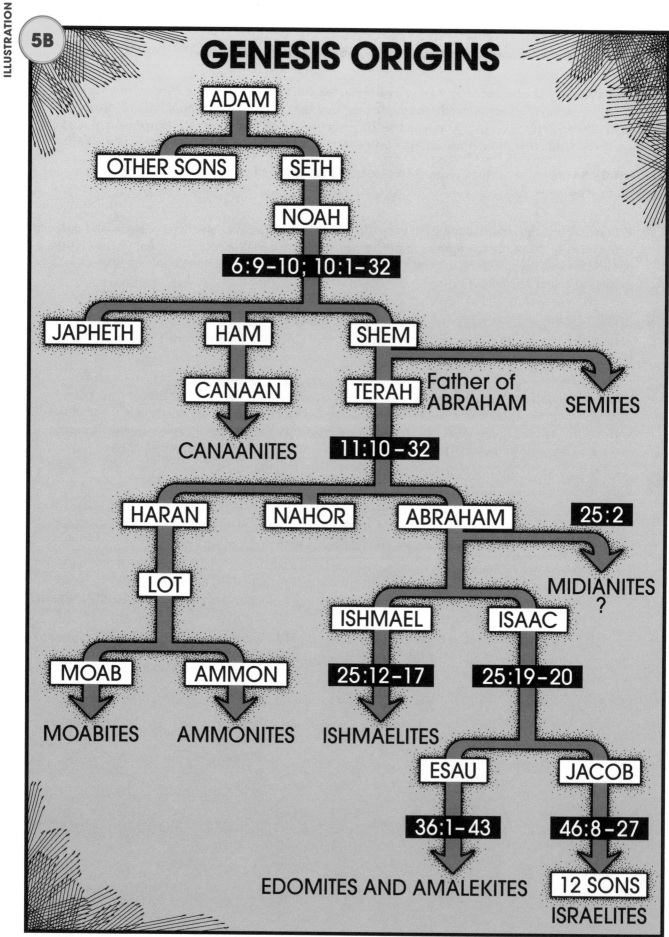

ADAM

OTHER SONS — SETH

NOAH

6:9–10; 10:1–32

JAPHETH — HAM — SHEM → SEMITES

CANAAN

TERAH — Father of ABRAHAM

CANAANITES

11:10–32

HARAN — NAHOR — ABRAHAM — 25:2

LOT

MIDIANITES?

ISHMAEL — ISAAC

MOAB — AMMON

25:12–17 — 25:19–20

MOABITES — AMMONITES — ISHMAELITES

ESAU — JACOB

36:1–43 — 46:8–27

EDOMITES AND AMALEKITES — 12 SONS

ISRAELITES

Although Genesis 12–16 refers to the first of the Chosen People as *Abram* and *Sarai*, Genesis 17:1–22 describes their names being changed to *Abraham* and *Sarah*. Abram means "exalted ancestor"; Abraham means "father of a multitude." Sarah, meaning "princess," is a variant of Sarai.

ILLUSTRATION 5B depicts the complex family tree found in the first book of the Old Testament.

1 Genesis gives information about **ADAM** (chs. 1–3), **ABRAHAM** (12:1–25:11), **ISAAC** and **JACOB** (25:12–36:43), and **JOSEPH** (37:1–50:26). These narratives contain more than mere basic history. They describe how the Chosen People increase in number, and eventually settle in Egypt. They also describe the origins of seven other nations living in and around Canaan—six of which have genetic links to Abraham (the Canaanites were descendants of Canaan, Noah's grandson, Gen. 9:18–27).

2 The origins of the Chosen People are traced from **ADAM** through **SETH**, **NOAH**, **SHEM**, **TERAH**, **ABRAHAM**, and **ISAAC** to **JACOB** (whose name is changed to *Israel*)—and finally to Jacob's twelve sons, the original **ISRAELITES**.

3 Genesis portrays the origins of seven neighboring nations, who (according to the biblical narrative) made life difficult for Israel.

   a. A curse is placed on **HAM**'s son, **CANAAN**, 9:18–29. The **CANAANITES** were living in the Promised Land when Joshua led the Israelites across the Jordan.

   b. The **MIDIANITES** were descendants of Midian, whom Abraham's second wife, Keturah, bore to him, Genesis 25:2; see Numbers 31:1–54.

   c. The origin of the **MOABITES** and **AMMONITES** is described negatively. They are the product of an incestuous relationship between a drunken **LOT** and his two daughters, 19:30–38.

   d. Genesis 16 refers to the birth of **ISHMAEL**. It hints that he and his descendants will be troublemakers, 16:11,12.

   e. **ESAU** was the first of the **EDOMITES**. The text suggests he was irresponsible (25:29–34), and unfeeling toward his parents, 26:34,35. Genesis 25:23 predicts that he will be subservient to his brother **JACOB**.

   f. Genesis also refers to the origins of the **AMALEKITES**, 36:12. Amalek's father, Eliphaz, was a son of **ESAU**. His mother, Timna, was a concubine of Eliphaz.

4 In summary, Genesis says:

   ● Much about the life of **ABRAHAM**, 12:1–25:11.

   ● Little about the life of **ISAAC**, 25:19–28:5.

   ● Much about the life of **JACOB**, 25:19–35:29.

   ● Much about the life of **JOSEPH**, 37:1–50:26.

These stories describe the origins and growth of the Chosen People, and explain how they first came to live in Egypt. They prepare the stage for the greatest of Old Testament events—**the Exodus from Egypt**.

1 Genesis contains numerous references to what God says He will do for Abraham and achieve through him, Genesis 12:1–3,7; 13:15; 15:18–20; 17:8. The covenant God makes with Abraham, a *Covenant of Divine Commitment*, is a one-way affair—from God to Abraham (**yellow figure**). In this covenant (depicted on the **white scroll** in the *lower section* of **ILLUSTRATION 5C**), God promises:

- To give Abraham and his descendants the **land of Canaan**;
- To give Abraham **offspring** and build a *nation* from him;
- To use Abraham and his descendants to bring *blessings to other nations* (depicted by the **contents of a cup over Canaan overflowing across the world**).

2 The narrative leaves the reader wondering whether God's promises to Abraham will ever be fulfilled. Some of the stories about Abraham and Sarah are full of suspense.

a. Abraham almost loses Sarah to another man, Genesis 12:10–20; 20:1–18.

b. If Lot had chosen Canaan instead of the Jordan Valley, Abraham would have lost his claim to the Promised Land, Genesis 13.

c. Although Abraham and Sarah wait 25 years for the birth of Isaac (Genesis 21), a few years after Isaac's birth, God tells Abraham to go to the land of Moriah to offer up Isaac as a sacrifice, Genesis 22. After God spares Abraham the agony of having to sacrifice Isaac, God provides Abraham with a ram which he then sacrifices. (Eventually, David bought a threshing floor in Jerusalem on which he offered a sacrifice, 2 Samuel 24:18–25. 2 Chronicles 3:1 states that Solomon eventually built the Temple on that site, and refers to it as Mt. Moriah. It is possible that the Chronicler wanted to ascribe an early origin to the royal shrine by identifying the unnamed hilltop formerly used as a threshing floor with the mountain where Abraham made prepared sacrifice his son. This link is made in the *Book of the Jubilees* 18:13, and in the writings of Josephus and Jewish rabbis.)

3 Other stories bring the behavior of Abraham and Sarah into question.

a. Both suggest resorting to alternative plans for obtaining an heir. Abraham suggests adoption, 15:1–6. Sarah suggests concubinage (Hagar, Sarah's handmaid, bore a child fathered by Abraham), ch. 16; 17:18.

b. Both laugh at God and suggest that the idea of the aged Sarah becoming pregnant is ridiculous, 17:17; 18:12. (The name *Isaac* means "laughter.")

Prior to Sarah's death, Abraham has one "chosen son" by her, and Isaac and Rebekah have produced two grandsons (Esau, Jacob) for him, Genesis 21 and 25:19–26. All that Abraham owns of Canaan is a field and a burial cave bought for 400 shekels of silver, ch. 23. After Sarah dies, Abraham takes another wife (Keturah, who bore him six sons) and some concubines, 25:1–11.

The promise concerning the land of Canaan is sealed in a solemn ceremony. God's presence (symbolized by a **smoking fire-pot and a flaming torch**) passes between animals that have been cut in two—an action that declares, "May the fate that has overtaken these animals overtake Me if I break My promise to you," Genesis 15:7–21. In the course of this ceremony, God assures Abraham that his descendants will indeed eventually get the land—in 400 years time. This promise began to come to pass after the Israelites entered Canaan under the leadership of Joshua, and came to completion during the reign of David.

Genesis 12:1–3 and v. 7 are essential to a proper understanding of the biblical narrative.

Now the Lord said to Abram, "Go from your country and your kindred and your father's house to the land that I will show you. I will make of you a great nation, and I will bless you, and make your name great, so that you will be a blessing. I will bless those who bless you, and the one who curses you I will curse; and in you all the families of the earth shall be blessed.

"To your offspring I will give this land."

Throughout the Bible's big story, *there is only one Hero, God—who always acts in grace.* To work through Genesis 12:1–25:10 is to be made very aware of the truths embedded in this statement.

Genesis 12:1-9

When making a covenant with Abraham (12:1–3), God commands him to go to the land that God will show him. The 75-year-old Abraham responds by gathering together his 65-year-old wife Sarah, his nephew Lot, all the possessions they have gathered, and all the persons they have "acquired" in Haran. They then travel south from Haran to Canaan. After entering Canaan, Abraham spends some time at Shechem, and finally settles between Bethel and Ai. He builds an altar and worships the Lord at both Shechem and the final stopping place between Bethel and Ai.

Genesis 12:10-20

Abraham and Sarah go to Egypt to seek relief from a famine. While there, Sarah finds herself in a rather awkward situation with the pharaoh. True, the (at least 65-year-old) ancestress of the Chosen People must have been rather beautiful, but the manner in which Abraham extricates himself and Sarah from the situation is not admirable, even though Sarah actually is his half-sister, 20:12. The point is: If the pharaoh had kept Sarah, she could not have produced offspring for Abraham. Cliff-hanger one!

Genesis 13

After escaping from the clutches of the pharaoh, the patriarchal community returns to Canaan where Abraham offers Lot, his nephew, a choice of where he wishes to live. Lot can live in either the region to the east of the Jordan River or in Canaan. It is sometimes suggested that Abraham showed generosity in giving Lot this choice. However, does Abraham really have authority to offer Lot the land God has promised to Abraham and his descendants? Had Lot decided that he wanted Canaan, Abraham would have lost the Promised Land! Fortunately, Lot chooses to live in the region to the east of the Jordan River. Cliff-hanger two!

Genesis 14

When Lot is captured by a coalition of five northern kings, Abraham rescues him. After rescuing Lot, Abraham surprisingly pays tithes to Melchizedek, who served as both king and priest at Salem (Jerusalem), 14:17–24. No laws concerning tithes have been given as yet. Is the narrative encouraging later Jews to pay their Temple tithe willingly and regularly—even as their ancestor Abraham did?

Genesis 15:1-6

Because Sarah has not been able to conceive a child, Abraham suggests to God that he adopt Eliezer as his son—Eliezer, a slave born in his house. God rejects the suggestion, and assures Abraham that he will eventually have many descendants—as many descendants as there are stars in the sky. (Tablets found at Nuzi in Mesopotamia state that a master could adopt a slave as his heir; however, the tablets stipulate that the adopted heir had to yield to a true son born later.)

Genesis 15:7–21

God then reminds Abraham that God brought him from Ur in Babylonia to give him the land of Canaan. Abraham responds by asking, "O Lord God, how am I to know that I shall possess it?" (15:8). A significant ritual follows. Abraham is told to get a heifer, a goat, a ram, a turtle dove, and a young pigeon. He then cuts the heifer, goat, and ram in two, and places the two sets of halves in two lines a short distance apart. The scene intensifies dramatically. The sun sets. Abraham falls into some kind of supernatural sleep. "Dread and great darkness" fall on him, and, while he is in this condition, God repeats the promise concerning land. Yes, all that God has promised Abraham will come to pass—but not quite yet. Before it comes to pass, Abraham's descendants will have to endure captivity and slavery in a strange land for four hundred years. So, patience, Abraham! Patience! Another cliff-hanger!

Then a smoking fire-pot and a flaming torch pass between the halves of the animals. The event is a covenant-making ritual. Fire, darkness, torch, light? In the Old Testament, these signify the presence of God, Genesis 1:2; Exodus 3:2, 13:21, 19:18; 20:21. In rituals such as those described in Genesis 15, the persons who make the promises pass between the halves of animals to declare their willingness to suffer the fate of the animals, should they break their promises. In Genesis 15, God alone passes between the animals—binding Himself to honor the promise to provide Abraham with land.

During this ceremony, God assures Abraham that his descendants will indeed eventually get the land—in 400 years time. This promise came to pass when, after God rescued the Israelites from Egypt and led them through the wilderness for forty years, the people entered the land under the leadership of Joshua.

Chapter 16

Ten years have now passed, and Abraham and Sarah have no children. Sarah gives her maid Hagar to Abraham, and suggests that he raise up progeny through her. Hagar conceives with little difficulty. However, when strife develops between Sarah and Hagar, Hagar is sent away—and eventually gives birth to Ishmael. God declares that Ishmael, the product of the union—and the father of the Arabs—will grow into a nation of considerable size and consist of twelve tribes, 16:10, 17:20. Even so, the Chosen People will develop from Isaac, whom God will eventually give to Abraham through Sarah, 17:21.

Genesis 17

Abram's name is now changed to Abraham, and Sarai's to Sarah. The practice of circumcision is introduced—to serve as a sign of the covenant relationship God has established with Abraham and his descendants. God then promises 99-year-old Abraham that his 89year-old wife will soon have a child! Abraham considers the suggestion impossible, laughs, and asks why Ishmael should not be seen as his successor, 17:16–21. God responds that the line of promise must go through the (as yet) unborn Isaac—not Ishmael. (Note that Ishmael was conceived while Abraham was in an uncircumcised state; however, Isaac was conceived after Abraham was circumcised, 17:22–27, 21:5.)

Genesis 18 and 19

The narrative speaks of Abraham and Sarah practicing hospitality toward three important visitors. When these guests tell Abraham that Sarah will soon conceive and bear a child, Sarah laughs. The visitors then tell Abraham of the fate that is about to overtake Sodom and Gomorrah. Abraham responds by doing some bargaining, in the hope that he might save these cities in which Lot's family resides. The matter is settled in God's way—not in the manner Abraham envisions. Sodom and Gomorrah are destroyed, and Lot's wife meets an unusual end, 19:26. The loss of his wife leaves Lot with two daughters, but no sons. His daughters take matters into their own hands to resolve the issue of male offspring, 19:30–38. They get their father drunk, have sex with him, and become pregnant by him. Each bears a son—the progenitors of the (eventually) hated and despised Moabites and Ammonites.

Genesis 20

Abraham and Sarah now pay a visit to the region of Gerar. When King Abimelech sees Sarah, he is so attracted to the 89-year-old that he decides to add her to his harem. However, God tells Abimelech that if he does that, he is as good as dead—a rather disturbing thought. So Abimelech hands Sarah back to Abraham and clears the way for Sarah to produce a child and heir for Abraham. The narrative resembles that of 12:10–18. On both occasions, Abraham emerges from the predicament much better off in terms of material possessions, 12:16, 20:14,16.

Later, we read of Isaac and Rebekah in a similar predicament—again, with Abimelech, king of the Philistines, at Gerar, 26:1–16. Some suggest that these incidents show the fate of the ancestresses—and therefore the hope of *offspring*—to be hanging in jeopardy. Again, cliff-hangers!

Genesis 21

Finally, the child of promise, Isaac, is born. In the midst of the rejoicing, Sarah's treatment of Hagar and Ishmael is rather shoddy, 21:1–21. It is left to God, the Hero throughout, to show mercy to Ishmael.

Genesis 22

A transformed Abraham now prepares to offer as a sacrifice to God the one son God has given him through Sarah. We are not told what his thoughts are on the way to the mount of sacrifice, or what he expects God to do. However, had God not intervened, and had Abraham's knife descended, there would have been no Chosen People. Another cliff-hanger! Abraham eventually sacrificed a ram instead of Isaac. It is possible that the Genesis narrative contains the subtext that the Israelites were not to practice child sacrifice, Leviticus 18:21 (but did! See Jeremiah 7:31, 19:5, 32:35; 2 Kings 17:17, 23:10).

Later Jewish writers linked the mount of sacrifice to the threshing floor which David bought from Araunah the Jebusite (2 Samuel 24:18–25), on which (according to 2 Chronicles 3:1) Solomon built the Jerusalem Temple. However, the *Samaritans* eventually linked the mount of sacrifice to Mt. Gerizim. Islam teaches that Ishmael, not Isaac, was the one being prepared for sacrifice—on Mount Moriah in Jerusalem where the Islamic shrine, the Dome of the Rock, now stands.

Genesis 23

When Sarah dies at the age of 127, Abraham is 137 years old, and Isaac is 37 years old. Although apparently the inhabitants of Canaan have permitted Abraham to live among them, he is still a wandering nomad and needs a place to bury his deceased wife. So he approaches the local citizens to buy a cave. They respond by paying him compliments about being a "mighty prince" and assure him that he can have any sepulcher he wants—*all for nothing*. But Abraham has in mind one particular burial place, the cave of Machpelah (*located in present-day Hebron*), and asks for permission to buy it at a fair price from its owner, Ephron the Hittite. Ephron now enters into the negotiations. He is willing to part with the cave, but he also insists on including the surrounding field in the deal, 23:11 (the first "package deal" in biblical history). Naturally there is loud talk about *giving* the cave and the field to Abraham: "I *give* you the field! I *give* you the cave." Abraham is willing to increase the size of his proposed purchase, but insists on preserving his oriental dignity by *paying* for the property, v. 13. Ephron's reply is beautiful: "A piece of land worth a *mere four hundred shekels of silver*? What is that between you and me?" Ephron has now let Abraham know how much he wants for the cave and land. Abraham agrees to the price, weighs it out, hands it over, and the land and cave are his. Abraham now owns part of the Promised Land, even if it is only a small corner—and even if it is bought for a price, rather than given freely by God. The burial cave becomes the final resting place of Sarah (23:19), Abraham (25:7–10), Isaac and Rebekah, and Jacob and Leah, Genesis 49:29, 50:13.

Genesis 23 makes vivid reading for tourists who have had financial dealings with some of the guides and traders in today's Middle East when inquiring about the price of an article or tour—only to be told: "But sir,

what is money between you and me? It is my honor and privilege to serve you. Let not such a thing as money be mentioned between us! Are we not both gentlemen?"

Genesis 24

Abraham finds a suitable wife (Rebekah) for his son, Isaac. The family line will continue.

Genesis 25

Abraham marries again. Apparently, he also acquires some concubines, 25:6. Although Keturah, his second wife, provides him with six children, Isaac remains his favored son, 25:5. Abraham's second marriage lasts 38 years. He dies at 175 and is buried by Isaac and Ishmael in the cave of Machpelah. It would seem that Abraham retained his sexual vitality throughout his life—a very important factor in the world of that day (and in many parts of the world still today). No doubt the fact that Abraham retained his potency into a ripe old age meant much to his descendants in a world where to lose potency was to lose validity and authority as a person, 1 Kings 1:1–5.

5A Genesis 1:1–12:3 outlines how, as the human family grew, God's focus of attention eventually centered on Abraham and Sarah, the first of a community that became known as the Chosen People. God did not call them because of what He saw *in them*. God called them because of what He planned to accomplish *through them*. He did not choose them for special privilege; He chose them for a special mission.

5B Genesis reveals details about a complex family tree. The line of the Chosen People did not always flow through the first-born; it went through Isaac—not Ishmael, and through Jacob—not Esau. The Genesis narrative also introduces seven nations (six of which had genetic links to Abraham) which the Israelites eventually viewed with disdain: the Canaanites, Midianites, Moabites, Ammonites, Ishmaelites, Edomites, and Amalekites. The Canaanites were descendants of Noah's grandson, Canaan, and were looked on as a cursed people, Genesis 9:25.

5C Genesis 12:1–3 describes God making a covenant with Abraham—a one-way Covenant of Divine Commitment in which God told Abraham:

- to go to the land of Canaan—which He would eventually give to Abraham and his descendants;
- that He would make out of Abraham a great and numerous people;
- that He would use him and his descendants to bring blessings to the nations of the world.

5D The narrative describing the life of Abraham and Sarah is detailed and complex.

- Although God had promised Abraham numerous offspring, at the end of his life the Chosen People consisted of Abraham (and Sarah), Isaac (and Rebekah), and Jacob.
- At times, Genesis describes the behavior of Abraham and Sarah as not exactly saintly, and it raises the question, "In what way were they to be a source of blessing to the nations?"
- Although God promised to give the land of Canaan to Abraham and his descendants, at the close of his life, Abraham owned only a field and a burial cave within its borders (*which he purchased*). Abraham and Sarah, Isaac and Rebekah, Jacob and Leah were eventually buried in that cave.

CROSS WAYS

1 SECTION

UNITS 1-10

From Creation to the Transjordan

UNIT 6

The World of the Patriarchs

The Frailties and Fortunes of Abraham's Offspring

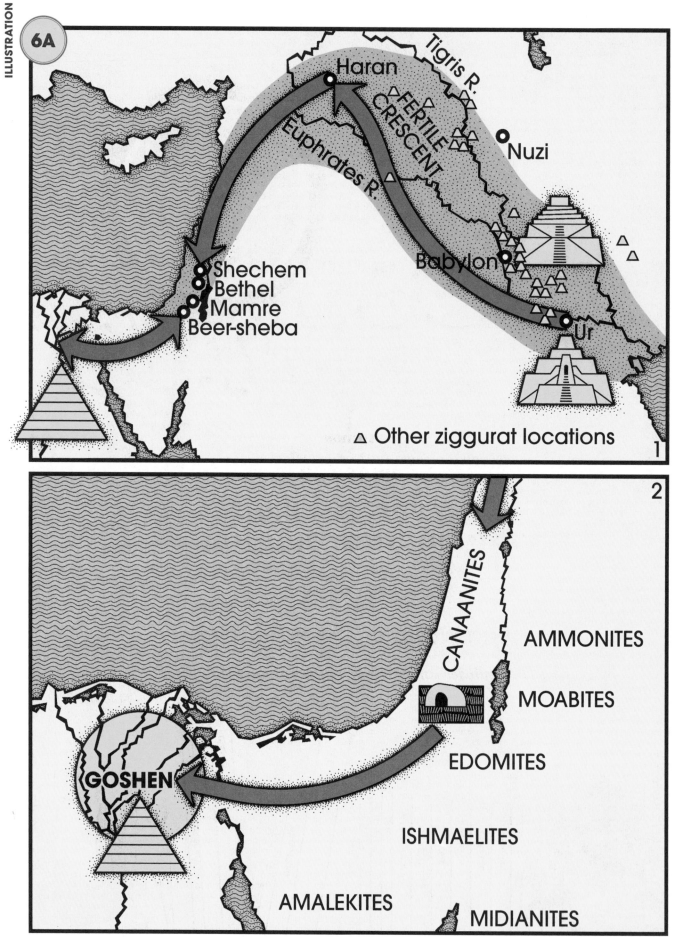

6A

Tigris R.

Haran

FERTILE CRESCENT

Nuzi

Euphrates R.

Shechem
Bethel
Mamre
Beer-sheba

Babylon

Ur

△ Other ziggurat locations

1

2

CANAANITES

AMMONITES

MOABITES

EDOMITES

GOSHEN

ISHMAELITES

AMALEKITES

MIDIANITES

Upper section

1. The **FERTILE CRESCENT** was aptly named. Much of it lay between, or near, the **Tigris** and **Euphrates Rivers**, and the fertility of its fields was enriched by the soil these rivers deposited during periods of flooding. The region between the Tigris and Euphrates was called *Mesopotamia*—a name derived from two Greek words meaning *Between the Rivers*.

2. Although Abraham's family roots were in **Ur of the Chaldees** (in present day Iraq), God called him after he settled in **Haran**, Genesis 11:31. The patriarchal narratives speak of Abraham traveling from Haran to *Canaan* (12:4–9), and from Canaan to *Egypt* (**pyramid**) and back, Genesis 12:12–20.

3. The Genesis narrative refers to Abraham, Isaac, and Jacob establishing and reestablishing shrines at **Shechem**, **Bethel**, **Mamre**, and **Beer-sheba**.

4. The city of **Nuzi** flourished in the middle centuries of the second millennium B.C. During excavations in A.D. 1925–31, thousands of stone tablets were found there. Their contents provide insights about the social customs that prevailed during the patriarchal age. (See 6D.)

5. The illustration depicts *ziggurats* (**tiered temple-towers**) near **Ur** and **Babylon**. It also contains **28 small symbols** to denote the localities of other ziggurats built in the region.

Lower section

At the close of the Genesis narrative, Abraham's descendants are happily settled in the region of **GOSHEN** in Egypt (**pyramid**). Although they have been promised the land of Canaan, they own only two things within its borders: a **field and a cave** which Abraham bought from Ephron the Hittite, Genesis 23.

Genesis describes, in unsavory terms, the origins of the nations that lived within and around Israel's borders. These narratives say to later generations, "Have as little as possible to do with those thorns-in-the-flesh. Remember their origins!" Much of Israel's history had to do with squabbles and wars with neighboring nations *who were their own relatives!*

1. Genesis 9:18–27 refers to *Canaan* (grandson of *Noah*) being cursed because of something *Ham*, his *father*, had done. Abraham's descendants continued to despise Canaan's descendants, the **CANAANITES**.

2. Genesis 19:30–38 states that the **AMMONITES** and **MOABITES** were the product of an incestuous relationship between a drunken Lot and his two daughters. The Israelites despised them.

3. The **EDOMITES** were descendants of Esau. Genesis 25:29–34, 26:34,35 and 27:40,46 refer to them in negative terms. Genesis 25:23 predicts that the descendants of Esau will serve the descendants of Jacob. Second Samuel 8:13,14 tells how David incorporated Edom into his realm in a brutal manner. To regain their freedom, the Edomites revolted from Solomon, 1 Kings 11:14–22; see Genesis 27:39,40. They helped Babylon destroy Judah in 587 B.C. The contents of the book of Obadiah constitute a bitter attack on the Edomites.

4. Genesis 16 describes the origin of Ishmael, the first of the **ISHMAELITES**. Ishmael was the son of Hagar, Sarah's handmaid. Abraham was his father. A hint about the character of Ishmael and his descendants is given in Genesis 16:12; note also 37:25–27 ("a wild donkey of a man").

5. Genesis 25:2 says that after Sarah's death, Abraham married Keturah. She bore him, among others, Midian. The relationship between the **MIDIANITES** and the Israelites was stressful, Genesis 37:28,36; Judges 6,7.

6. Genesis 36:12 refers to the birth of Amalek, the product of a union between Esau's son Eliphaz and his concubine Timna (hence, Esau's grandson). The Israelites despised the **AMALEKITES**, Exodus 17:8–16; Deuteronomy 25:17–19; Judges 6:3; 1 Samuel 15:1–9, 27:8–12.

The Genesis narrative describes the origins of seven neighboring nations whom the Israelites despised. It is important to note the reference to *seven* enemy nations in Deuteronomy 7:1, Joshua 3:10 and Ezekiel 25–32. Paul refers to *seven* nations when preaching in Antioch, Acts 13:19. When Jesus fed 4,000 men in the *Gentile* region of the Decapolis (Mark 7:31, 8:1–10), there were *seven* baskets of left-overs. Most likely, in this second feeding miracle (see Mark 6:30–44), *Jesus is declaring compassion for the Gentiles.*

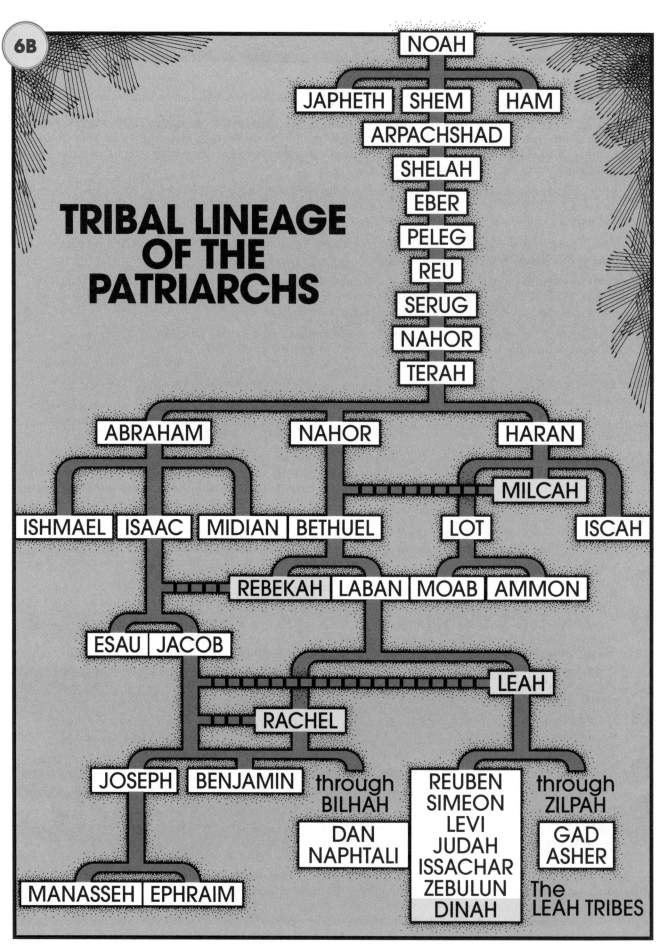

6B

TRIBAL LINEAGE OF THE PATRIARCHS

Genesis 24 describes Abraham's efforts to ensure that Isaac will have a suitable wife from an acceptable background. The family tree must not be contaminated by marriage to a Canaanite! Hence, Abraham places his servant under oath (24:2–4) and sends him to find a bride for Isaac from among "pure" relatives.

Rebekah shows a similar concern when seeking a wife for Jacob. Isaac agrees with her, forbids his son to take a wife from among the Canaanites, and sends him to Mesopotamia to find both a female and a fortune, Genesis 27:46–28:5. Jacob returns with two wives, two concubines, twelve sons, and one daughter, 34:1.

ILLUSTRATION 6B depicts the "marriage mix" that took place among the descendants of **TERAH**.

1 Terah, a 10th generation descendant of **NOAH**, had three sons, **ABRAHAM**, **NAHOR**, and **HARAN**, Genesis 11:26.

2 Haran, who died in Ur of the Chaldees, predeceased his father, Terah—and therefore was not among those who migrated from Ur to the city of Haran, 11:28,31,32.

3 **LOT** was a son of Haran, 11:31.

4 Haran's daughter, **MILCAH**, married her uncle, Nahor, 11:29. Their son, **BETHUEL**, was the father of **REBEKAH** and **LABAN**, 24:24,29.

5 Rebekah married Abraham's son, **ISAAC**, 24:62–67. Their marriage produced **ESAU** and **JACOB**, 25:19–26.

6 Jacob married two cousins, **LEAH** and **RACHEL**—daughters of his uncle, Laban, 29:1–30. He also took as concubines the handmaids of Leah (**ZILPAH**) and Rachel (**BILHAH**), 30:1–9.

7 Leah bore Jacob six sons and one daughter (**DINAH**). Rachel, Zilpah, and Bilhah each bore Jacob two sons.

The life of Abraham is outlined in Genesis 12:1–25:18. The patriarchal history continues in the subsequent narrative.

- *Isaac*, 25:19–28:9; his death is reported in 35:27–29.
- *Jacob*, 25:19–37:1. He is referred to frequently in the Joseph narrative. His last days are reported in chs. 49,50.
- *Joseph*, 37:1–50:26

THE ISAAC NARRATIVE

The Isaac narrative serves as a transition from the Abraham narrative to the Jacob narrative.

 Genesis 22 describes the contemplated sacrifice of Isaac, in which Isaac plays a passive role.

 Genesis 24:1–67 describes Abraham getting a wife for Isaac from his extended family still living in Mesopotamia; see Genesis 11:31. The narrative describing Abraham's servant persuading Laban to permit his sister, Rebekah, to marry Isaac is colorful. Rebekah bears Isaac two sons, Esau and Jacob, Genesis 25:19–26.

 The narrative offers a prophetic hint that Jacob will triumph over his older brother, Esau. After all, Esau eventually acted very irresponsibly; he sold his *birthright* to Jacob for a crust of bread and a pot of stew, Genesis 25:28–34.

 Later, Rebekah manipulates things to ensure that Jacob, not Esau, inherits Isaac's blessing, 27:1–40. (Deuteronomy 21:15–17 states that the son who possessed the birthright was to receive a double share of the family inheritance when the head of the house died.)

Why did not Isaac, on discovering Jacob's deception, retract his words to the younger son and set the record straight? It was believed that when a word of blessing or curse was spoken, that word went forth with power to accomplish its message. It could not be recalled or retracted. Later chapters suggest that Jacob not only regretted his actions in this sordid incident, but reaped the consequences of his deed.

 Jacob becomes the key player in the drama that follows—some of which focuses on the continuing conflict between the two brothers.

Genesis 32:3–33:17 describes the final confrontation between Jacob and Esau that took place years later. The scene ends happily; the brothers are reconciled.

THE JACOB NARRATIVE

Although the Jacob narrative contains disturbing details, modern readers need to note:

The challenge is to *understand* Jacob's actions, not *agree* with them. The writer's goal is not to tell a story about a saint, but to capture the reader's attention with a narrative whose outcome hangs in doubt throughout.

The narratives in Genesis 25:23–26, 23:34, 27:1–45, and 32:3–33:17 could be classified as "conflict stories." They point to ongoing struggles between the Israelites and their Mesopotamian ancestors, and between the Israelites and the Edomites.

Other important details in the Jacob narrative are the following:

    a. Genesis 26:1–11 tells of the second ancestress, Rebekah, finding herself in a situation similar to that in which her mother-in-law, Sarah, had found herself on two previous occasions; see Genesis 12:10–20 and ch. 20.

b. Genesis 26:12–33 describes a dispute over a water supply; Genesis 21:22–34 speaks of a similar incident in relation to Abraham. The point seems to be that although the Chosen People do not own much of the Promised Land by the close of the Genesis narrative, they do own a tiny portion of it (Genesis 23), plus some water rights.

c. Genesis 26:34,35 refers to Esau's undesirable marriages. In the narrative that follows Genesis 28, Jacob heads north to the regions from which his grandfather Abraham had come much earlier. Two reasons are given for this journey:

- To escape the anger of his brother Esau (27:41–45), and

- To find a wife who would receive greater parental approval than that given to those Esau had chosen, 27:46–28:5.

d. During the journey north, Jacob has a remarkable encounter with God at Bethel, Genesis 28. In a dream, Jacob sees God speaking to him from the top of a ladder reaching up into the heavens, reassuring him that the promises made to Abraham will be fulfilled in him.

e. After Jacob arrives at Haran, he establishes a harem of two wives and two maids and develops a family (chs. 29,30), has difficulties with father-in-law Laban, decides to flee from Laban and return to the Promised Land, (ch. 31), and is reconciled to his brother Esau, chs. 32,33.

f. Genesis 34 describes the brutal manner in which Jacob's sons vindicate their sister Dinah's loss of honor.

g. Chapter 35 describes Jacob's journey to Mamre, the birth of Benjamin and the death of Rachel, Jacob's eventual meeting with Isaac, and Isaac's death.

h. Genesis 36 describes the growth of Esau's clan and their taking control of land to the east of Canaan.

THE JOSEPH NARRATIVE

The Joseph cycle begins in Genesis 37 and continues in one sweep to the close of Genesis—with one interruption: references to Judah's marriage to Shua, their three sons Er, Onan, and Shelah, and the question of responsibility for caring for Tamar, Er's widow (Genesis 38; see Deuteronomy 25:5–10).

Although the details of the Joseph narrative are well known, a couple of observations about their style are worthy of note.

- The Joseph cycle of stories possesses a unified, dramatic quality, and in places is emotionally stirring. Each step of the plot lays the groundwork for the next event. It tells how a lowly Palestinian shepherd became the second most powerful official in Egypt. The narrative contains numerous events of high drama: Joseph in Egypt in the presence of long-not-seen brothers searching for food, Genesis 42:7–44:17; Judah's speech, 44:18–34; Joseph's final revealing of his identity, ch. 45.

- The Joseph cycle contains elements of a *wisdom narrative*. To illustrate, when Joseph first appears on the scene, he is something of a spoiled brat, finds himself forced to endure a series of difficult events, but grows in stature through the process. These events include resisting the sexual advances of a scheming woman, suffering patiently during an unjust imprisonment, interpreting dreams, exercising sound judgment in high office, and handling the dilemma of determining what to do with possibly unrepentant brothers. When it is all over, Joseph declares, "for God sent me before you to preserve life," and, "it was not you who sent me here but God," Genesis 45:5,7.

At the heart of these patriarchal narratives is the conviction that God intervenes in human history to accomplish divine purposes. God's hand is detected not only in supernatural appearances, visions, and awe-inspiring wonders (very few of which occur in the Joseph stories), but also in the seemingly detached decisions of humanity. God weaves these decisions neatly into His overall plan for humanity. Through actions which outwardly appear to be evil, God works without show or fanfare, often in ways beyond the ability of the human mind to perceive, to draw good from evil and to make sense out of the seemingly senseless. The patriarchal narratives show how the promises first made to Abraham were passed on and treasured, and how the Chosen People, eventually called out of Egypt and gathered around Sinai, first settled in Egypt.

The Genesis narrative closes with a question: What has happened to the promise to Israel that it would be a great people in possession of Canaan? The reader is left with the clear impression that God's work, as great as it has been to date, is not yet finished.

The World of The Patriarchs

Several centuries ago, scholars began suggesting that the patriarchs never existed, but were the imaginative product of later generations seeking to explain their origins and their unique place in the world. This theory gives little credence to the inspiration of Scripture. Furthermore, it surfaced at a time when little was known about the world of the Ancient Near East.

Archaeological work done during the past century indicates that Genesis reflects conditions and customs tthat prevailed in the Mesopotamian world of the patriarchs during the second millennium B.C.

1   Tablets unearthed at Nuzi reveal much about ancient marriage customs.

- A wife who was also a sister, either by blood or adoption, enjoyed a privileged status, Genesis 12:13; 20:12.
- A wife could give her maid to her husband and claim the offspring as her own, Genesis 16:1,2; 30:3,9. A contract found at Nuzi obliges a wife to do just that if she herself does not bear children, and adds that the offspring of the slave may not be cast out. (Note Abraham's prolonged hesitation when Sarah demands the expulsion of Hagar and Ishmael, Genesis 21:8–14.)
- If a maid became pregnant by her master, she was not to claim equality with her mistress, Genesis 16:4,5.
- The offspring of a maid could either inherit some of the family property with the children of the master's wife, or be set free, Genesis 21:10.

2   Other documents from the area tell of the sale of a birthright for three sheep, Genesis 25:29–34.

3   The possession of the family idols established title to the family inheritance, and the idols were given to the heirs when family property rights were transferred. Genesis 31:19, 33–35 ridicules idols and the practice of idolatry.

4   Ancient animal breeders believed that a female's offspring was affected by what the mother animal saw at the time of mating. Genesis 30:37–43 describes Jacob making use of this strategy to procure striped and speckled goats.

5   When people ate as guests in someone's house, the host had to guarantee their safety, Genesis 19:6–8. (This custom still exists in the Middle East today.)

6   Because water was often in short supply, nomads insisted that all who had right of access to a well be present when the well was opened, to ensure an equitable distribution of its contents, Genesis 29:8.

7   The presence of a few wicked individuals in a community contaminated the entire community; this principle, in reverse form, is referred to in Genesis 18.

The patriarchal narratives concern themselves, not merely with theological speculation, but with the nitty-gritty details of life in the world at the time of the patriarchs.

6A The region between the Tigris and Euphrates was fertile, and dotted with many temples referred to as ziggurats. After Terah and two of his sons, Nahor and Abraham, moved from Ur to Haran, God called Abraham and told him to go to the land of Canaan. Abraham, Isaac, and Jacob worshiped at shrines established in Shechem, Bethel, Mamre, and Beer-sheba. During a period of drought in Canaan, Abraham and Sarah spent time in Egypt.

After Jacob's son, Joseph, was sold into slavery in Egypt, Joseph rose to a position of power and prominence. Eventually, Jacob and his entire family moved to and settled in Egypt.

6B A complex family tree surfaces within the Genesis narrative. The line of the Old Testament Chosen People is traced through Abraham, Isaac, and Jacob and his twelve sons.

6C The Genesis narrative contains detailed accounts of the lives of Abraham, Isaac, and Jacob and his twelve sons (Joseph in particular). Although God did not always act with the speed His people might have desired, He had a timetable for getting things done. God repeated to each of the patriarchs the promises made to Abraham, and the promises eventually came to pass. The patriarchal/matriarchal narratives set the stage for the exodus from Egypt under Moses.

6D Archaeological discoveries made during recent centuries provide insights into the significance of some of the details contained in the patriarchal narratives.

CROSS WAYS®

1 SECTION

UNITS 1–10

From Creation to the Transjordan

UNIT 7
The Exodus from Egypt

The Exodus, the Big Event

GENESIS
JOSHUA
RUTH
1 SAMUEL
2 SAMUEL
1 KINGS
2 KINGS
1 CHRONICLES
2 CHRONICLES
EZRA
NEHEMIAH
ESTHER
JOB
PSALMS
PROVERBS
ECCLESIASTES
SONG OF SOLOMON
ISAIAH
JEREMIAH
LAMENTATIONS
EZEKIEL
HOSEA
JOEL
AMOS
OBADIAH
JONAH

7A

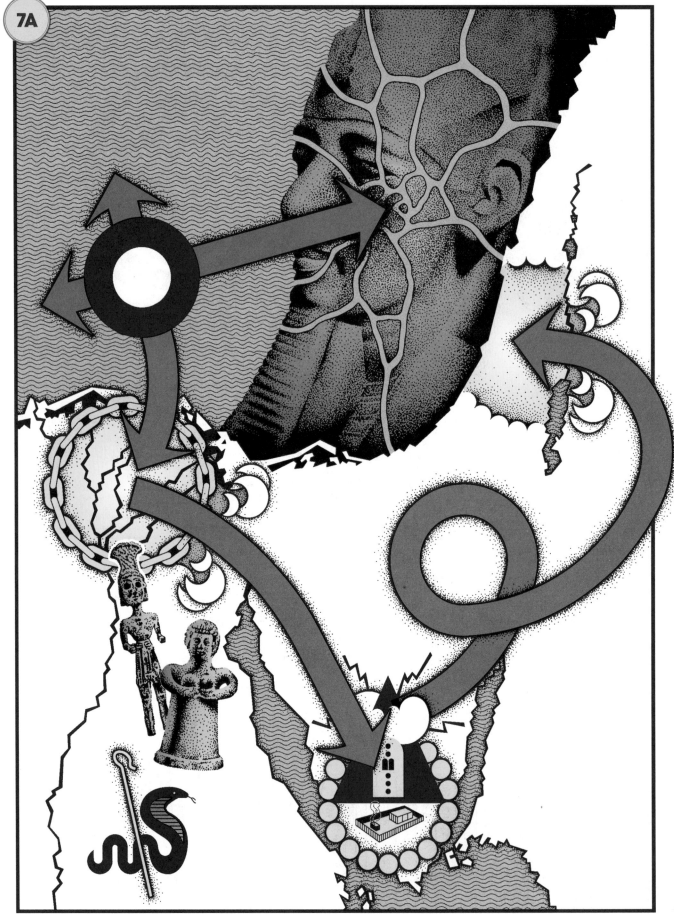

In the closing chapters of Genesis, Jacob and his descendants are happily settled in Egypt. They are not as yet a great nation. Although God has promised them possession of the land of Canaan, they own only a field within which is a burial cave.

In the opening chapters of Exodus, the curtain goes up on a scene several hundred years later than those outlined in the closing chapters of Genesis—a scene that anticipates the Exodus event. In Egypt, there came to power a pharaoh who "did not know Joseph," i.e., who forgot Joseph's services to the nation, Exodus 1:8.

ILLUSTRATION 7A summarizes events associated with the Exodus.

1. *Circle of chains around the Nile Delta:* Because the pharaoh was worried about Israel's increase in numbers, he tried to destroy the nation in two ways:
   - By enslaving the Israelites, Exodus 1:9–14;
   - By ordering midwives to kill all male infants born to them, Exodus 1:15–22.

2. *Idols:* The Israelites were worshiping false gods in Egypt, Joshua 24:14,15, Ezekiel 20:1–8a.

3. *Staff and serpent:* When Moses and Aaron first confronted the Egyptian magicians, both sides cast rods to the ground. A rod was an important symbol of authority. All the rods became snakes— but Aaron's rod-become-serpent swallowed the Egyptian rods-become-serpents, Exodus 7:8–13. *The God of Israel has power and authority over all other so-called gods!*

4. *Arrow from the symbol for God pointing to the pharaoh's face:* In the ten plagues that followed the encounter between Moses and Aaron and the Egyptian magicians, God fought a Holy War with the Egyptian pharaoh, 7:8–11:10.

5. *Waves, and arrow through chains and waves; arrow points to Mt. Sinai:* God opened up the waters to rescue His people from bondage in Egypt (Exodus 14:19–22), destroyed the Egyptian army (14:23–31), and led the Israelites to the region of Mt. Sinai, 15:22–19:1.

6. *Circle of dots around Mt. Sinai, cloud and lightning at its summit:* God gathered the Israelites around Mt. Sinai and revealed His presence at its summit by means of darkness, lightning, and a cloud, Exodus 19:2–25.

7. *Covenant symbol on Mt. Sinai:* God made a covenant with Israel at Sinai, Exodus 20:1–21. In the covenant, God told the people who He is, reminded them that He had rescued them from Egypt (20:1,2) and called them to respond in obedience. The covenant had six sections (*five dots, symbol for law-codes at position 3*). The commandments were guidelines for saying *thank You* to God for His goodness, and for *living in community.*

8. *Tabernacle beneath Mt. Sinai:* Exodus 25–31 and 35–40 describe the building of the Tabernacle and God taking up residence within it.

9. *Looped red arrow:* The Israelites spent nearly a year in the vicinity of Mt. Sinai (Exodus 19:1– Numbers 10:11). God then led them on an additional 39-year *journey through the arid Sinai wilderness.*

10. *Arrow through opened water of Jordan River:* Finally, God made it possible for the Israelites to pass through the Jordan River and enter the Promised Land, Joshua 3.

11. *Spiked yellow area:* After crossing the Jordan River, the Israelites strived to gain possession of the Promised Land by destroying the Canaanites living within its borders, Joshua 6–11.

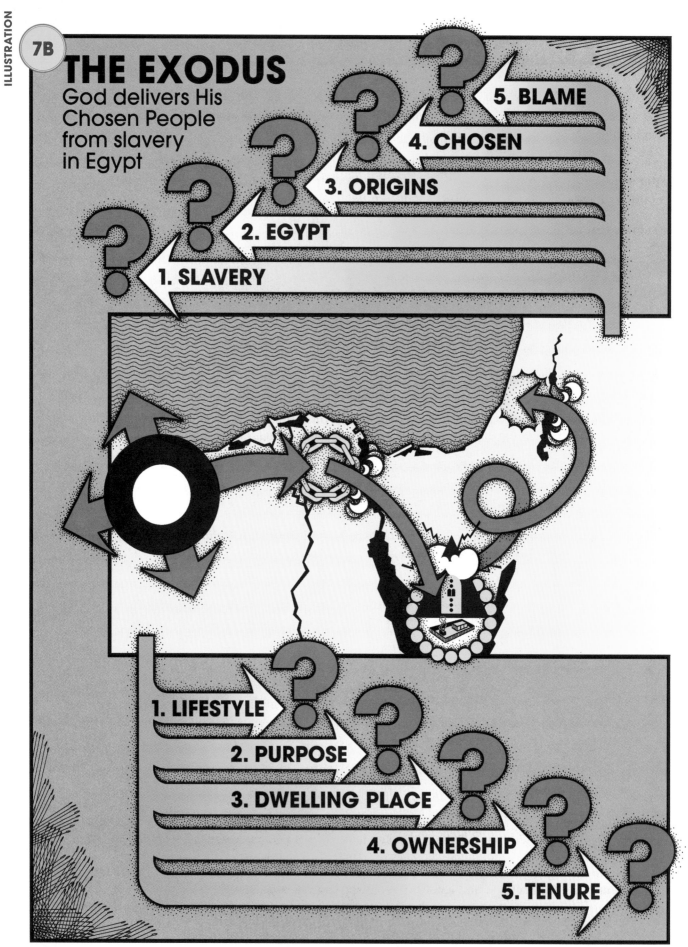

THE EXODUS
God delivers His Chosen People from slavery in Egypt

5. BLAME

4. CHOSEN

3. ORIGINS

2. EGYPT

1. SLAVERY

1. LIFESTYLE

2. PURPOSE

3. DWELLING PLACE

4. OWNERSHIP

5. TENURE

In the Exodus, God delivered the Israelites from slavery in Egypt. The memory of this pivotal event played a central role in Israel's worship life. **ILLUSTRATION 7B** depicts *the questions the ancient Israelites asked in relation to what preceded and followed the Exodus.*

LOOKING BACKWARD

1   *Question:*   ***Why are we, God's people, in SLAVERY?***
     Answer: A pharaoh arose who forgot Joseph.

2   *Question:*   ***Why are we living in EGYPT?***
     Answer: We settled there during the time of Joseph and Jacob.

3   *Question:*   ***What are our ORIGINS?***
     Answer: We are descendants of Abraham, the first of a Chosen People.

4   *Question:*   ***Why are we God's Chosen PEOPLE?***
     Answer: We were not chosen for privilege, but for mission. God chose us, in grace, to be a living reflection of His original plan for humanity (as described in Genesis 2–11).

5   *Question:*   ***Is God in any way to BLAME for the present moral confusion and chaos?***
     Answer: Certainly not! God made everything good, Genesis 1.

LOOKING FORWARD

1   *Question:*   ***What LIFESTYLE are we to pursue as we carry out God's mission?***
     Answer: The law-codes revealed in Exodus, Leviticus, Numbers, and Deuteronomy give us guidelines for copying God's own behavior patterns in our life together.

2   *Question:*   ***What PURPOSE (role) is our lifestyle to play among the nations?***
     Answer: It is to serve as a magnet to attract others into the community of Israel, Deuteronomy 4:1–8; Jeremiah 4:1,2.

3   *Question:*   ***Where is our final DWELLING PLACE to be ?***
     Answer: The land of Canaan.

4   *Question:*   ***To whom are we to ascribe OWNERSHIP of the Promised Land?***
     Answer: God! We Israelites are to look on ourselves as merely tenants in God's land, Jeremiah 2:7,15; Hosea 9:3.

5   *Question:*   ***How long can we expect to remain in the land—to have TENURE within its borders?***
     Answer: That depends on how seriously we take the stipulations of the Sinai Covenant, Deuteronomy 28:15–68.

The issues these questions raise played a crucial role in the history of Israel beyond the Exodus.

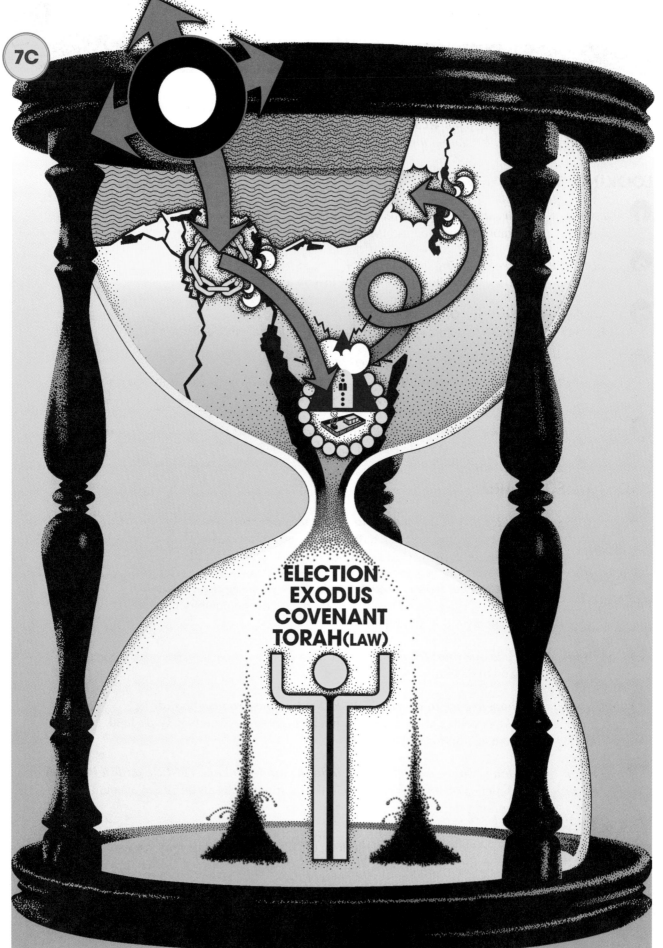

ELECTION
EXODUS
COVENANT
TORAH(LAW)

Recalling and "Re-membering"

How many actually participated in the Exodus from Egypt?

According to Exodus 12:37, 600,000 men on foot, besides children (and most certainly women!). Exodus 12:38 adds, "A mixed crowd also went up with them, and livestock in great numbers, both flocks and herds." In *Ancient Israel's Faith and History* (Louisville: Westminster John Knox Press, 2001, p.52), biblical scholar George Mendenhall writes:

> If the exodus group comprised 600,000 young men, then the whole group (including women, children, and older men) would have totaled two or three million people. This is implausibly high. Marched twenty-five abreast, this many people would form a column almost two hundred miles long, meaning that the front of the line would have reached Mount Sinai before the back of the line had left Egypt.

The following comments help understand the Jewish approach to remembering past events.

- In 1620, the Pilgrim Fathers came to the United States on the *Mayflower*. In 1770, Captain James Cook, aboard the *Endeavor*, explored the east coast of Australia and claimed it for England. Was anyone who is living today aboard the *Mayflower* or the *Endeavor*? We say, "No! Life began for us only during the past century. We did not take part in events that took place hundreds of years ago." When people who live in the Western world think about past events, they remember them in the sense of *recalling* them.

- When the ancient Israelites thought about past events, they did not merely *recall* them. They saw themselves as having *participated* in them. For example, when they offered their first fruits to God, they confessed the following creed:

You shall make response before the LORD your God, "A wandering Aramean [Jacob] was my father; <u>he</u> went down into Egypt and lived there as an alien, few in number; and there <u>he</u> became a nation great, mighty and populous. When the Egyptians treated <u>us</u> harshly and afflicted <u>us</u>, by imposing hard labor on <u>us</u>, <u>we</u> cried to the LORD, the God of our ancestors; the LORD heard <u>our</u> voice, and saw <u>our</u> affliction, <u>our</u> toil, and <u>our</u> oppression. The LORD brought <u>us</u> out of Egypt with a mighty hand and an outstretched arm, with a terrifying display of power, with signs and wonders; and He brought <u>us</u> into this place and gave <u>us</u> this land, a land flowing with milk and honey." (Deuteronomy 26:5–9)

  The words underlined above emphasize the change that takes place in the creed from *third* to *first* person. The <u>he</u> becomes <u>we</u>, <u>us</u>, and <u>our</u>. The passage illustrates vividly how the ancient Israelites saw themselves as having participated in past events. Although only some hundreds or several thousand Israelites might have taken part in the actual Exodus event, still today all Jewish people continue to celebrate their participation in this ancient event. The Old Testament commands them to "re-member" in this manner, Deuteronomy 6:20–25; Joshua 4:19–24.

ILLUSTRATION 7C makes use of an hourglass to depict how the ancient Israelites understood themselves as being "membered to" past events. They saw the sands of *past events* (***Exodus from Egypt***, *upper section*) flow around their *present history* (***person***, *lower section*).

Throughout their history, the Jewish people have celebrated their belief that:

- They are God's Chosen People (***ELECTION***);
- God rescued them from Egypt in the ***EXODUS*** event;
- God made a ***COVENANT*** with them at Mt. Sinai;
- God gave them the ***TORAH (LAW)***—Genesis, Exodus, Leviticus, Numbers, Deuteronomy—at Mt. Sinai.

The beginnings of Egyptian government go back to the fourth millennium B.C. By the time the children of Israel first settled in Egypt, the great sphinx (located near today's Cairo) was already ancient. Early in Egypt's history the two parts of the land, *Upper Egypt* (the *southern* part, stretched out along the Nile) and *Lower Egypt* (the *northern* part, mainly the delta area) were united. The terms Upper and Lower have to do with *height above sea level*, not with *north* and *south*. Egypt called itself "The Land of the Two Kingdoms." One pharaoh ruled both parts, except in times of weakness and division.

 During the 21st–18th centuries B.C. Egyptian power waned, owing to internal strife and invasions from the region of Mesopotamia. Waves of foreign invaders settled within Egypt's borders, first in the delta region and later in the rest of the land. These invaders were known as the Hyksos, or "foreign chieftains"; the pharaohs of the 15th and 16th dynasties came from the Hyksos. They set up their capital at Avaris in the delta region, and from there ruled not only Egypt but also much of Israel and Syria. During the period that the Hyksos ruled, the legitimate Egyptian rulers moved south to Thebes (present-day Luxor) in Upper Egypt.

Some historians suggest that the Israelites settled in Egypt while the Hyksos pharaohs ruled the land. Joseph's rise to power, and the favored treatment given to the members of Jacob's family, are more understandable if this was so. The Israelite' eventual fall from favor is also more understandable if their initial good fortune was in any way connected with the presence of the Hyksos.

As time went by, members of the traditional Egyptian nobility at Thebes drove out the Hyksos and regained control of the land. Rameses II (1290–1224) eventually moved the capital back to Avaris and renamed it Rameses. He also set in motion an intensive building program. Egyptian texts report that state slaves worked on these projects. Exodus 1:11 says that Israelites were involved in building projects at Pithom and Rameses. Exodus also says that Moses had frequent interviews with the pharaoh, which suggests that in Moses' time the capital was in the delta region where the Israelites lived.

HELPLESS ISRAEL

The opening chapter of Exodus gives the impression that God has forgotten His people and His plan. After all, the descendants of Abraham, the Chosen People, are now in a strange land. Their situation is a sad one. A pharaoh who did not know about Joseph now rules Egypt, Exodus 1:8. He notes the rapid growth in numbers of Abraham's descendants, is alarmed, and takes action. He enslaves them (Exodus 1:10–14) and demands the cooperation of Hebrew midwives in a program of genocide, 1:15–19. When the midwives ignore his instruction, he takes more drastic steps to deal with the Hebrew threat. He gives orders that all newly born Israelite boys be thrown into the Nile, 1:22.

Where is God in all of this? God is still around, and He is preparing for His "finest hour" in the history of the Israelites. God is about to lead His people into the land promised to the patriarchs. There is something remarkable in the way God accomplishes His plans for Israel. God does not call down the mighty armies of Egypt's northern neighbors. He raises up one man, Moses, equips him with divine courage, and sends him forth to do battle with the most powerful ruler in the world at that time. God made the ancient promises. God carries them out. God, and God alone, delivers Israel. To God alone be the glory!

MOSES, GOD'S INSTRUMENT

Exodus 2–4 tells of Moses' birth and upbringing, his flight from Egypt, and his call by God to be the instrument to deliver Israel from slavery. Initially, Moses was anything but enthusiastic about getting involved in God's plan. He was sure that people would not believe that God had appeared to him,

and that the Hebrew people would not accept him. Even after the Lord provided Moses with signs to substantiate his story and authority, he still held back. After all, Moses insisted that he was not an eloquent speaker! Moses submitted only when God agreed to send Aaron along with him to do the talking. Although the initial response of the people to Moses and Aaron was encouraging (Exodus 4:31), they were not always so enthusiastic about God's ways with them.

2. God confronted and commissioned Moses at Mt. Sinai (or Horeb), Exodus 3. Moses' questions concerning God's name (3:13,14) point to the significance of the use of names in the Ancient Near East. In the world of that time, a name was more than a label. It was part of the person, almost an extension of a person, and reflected that person's nature. To know someone's name was to have a certain power over that individual. Possibly Moses' curiosity was born of his desire to have some kind of security in his role as God's emissary.

3. Some translate the divine name which God revealed to Moses as "He causes to be what exists"; others translate it as "He will be," "He is present," or "I am Who I am." Some suggest that God's answer is a refusal to answer and a declaration that God is beyond naming—and therefore beyond humankind's power to control. God is to be known, not by any *name*, but by His *actions*—in particular by His actions in relation to Israel's history, Exodus 20:2.

THE CONTEST WITH PHARAOH

1. In the Ancient Near Eastern world, each nation had its own gods. These gods lived within the borders of the land over which they had authority, 1 Samuel 26:20. Nations related military successes to the respective strength of their own gods. When one nation conquered another, the victor put its gods into the national temple of the vanquished nation to declare publicly that its gods were the more powerful, 1 Samuel 5:1,2. This latter practice embarrassed more than one Israelite king, and moved some to practice a little syncretism to keep the victor happy.

2. The Egyptians believed that the pharaoh was more than mortal. They revered him as the embodiment of the deity, the divine son of the supreme god of Egypt, the sun-god Ra or Amon, and believed he possessed superhuman wisdom and power. A typical letter to a pharaoh could begin: "To my king, my lord, my sun-god." In challenging the pharaoh, God was not merely taking on an earthly ruler. God was taking on the gods of the most powerful nation in the world of that time and doing battle with them.

3. To a large degree, ancient non-Israelite religions concerned themselves with the control of nature. The issue in the ten plagues was more than, "How did they happen?" The issue was, "Who really controls nature in the land of Egypt?"

4. The Exodus events stated: When God took up the cause of a small, insignificant, oppressed, enslaved nation, no one on earth could stand in God's way. The God of Israel was not some second-rate deity confined to some obscure land. The God of Israel controlled nature and history in Egypt and in Israel—and indeed the whole world, Exodus 9:29. It is therefore not surprising that the pharaoh and his magicians could not control nature in Egypt.

THE TEN PLAGUES

1. The pharaoh is progressively cut down to size. In the beginning, his magicians keep pace with Moses and Aaron. Yes, the Egyptian magicians can turn their rods into serpents, 7:11–13. Yes, they can also turn the Nile into blood, 7:22. They can even call forth frogs, 8:7. However, they can never reverse anything that God does through Moses and Aaron. Pharaoh has to appeal to the opposition party to get rid of the frogs (8:8), which ironically were a symbol of life-giving power in Egypt.

2. Things go from bad to worse when even the pharaoh's magicians are attacked by the gnats (8:18) and by boils, 9:11. One can be forgiven for imagining that, from that point on, they were too busy trying to get relief by scratching themselves to offer much competition to Moses and Aaron. They beg the pharaoh to relent and yield. But this stubborn ruler persists in his private war with God, only to be ground progressively lower and lower into the dust—until finally Moses confronts him with a demand for animals for the *Israelites* to use in worshiping the Lord in the wilderness, 10:25. The pharaoh's "No!" to this request brings on a final, devastating plague (11:1–12:51) and results in the overthrow of the Egyptian forces.

3. The Israelites celebrated the Passover for the first time the night the Lord smote the first-born in Egypt and "passed over" the houses of God's people. This observance was to be repeated each year. Its purpose was (and is) to remember the Exodus. It was to be observed as a family feast, to be centered around the sacrifice of an unblemished lamb, roasted whole. This feast remains the most important observance in Israel's religious life. It reminds the Jewish people of the miraculous event in which God delivered them from bondage to be God's own special people, Exodus 12; Deuteronomy 6:20–25.

4 The ten plagues consisted of the following:

- Water turned into blood, Exodus 7:14–25;
- A plague of frogs, 8:1–15;
- A plague of gnats, 8:16–19;
- A plague of flies, 8:20–32;
- All livestock afflicted with disease, 9:1–7;
- A plague of boils, 9:8–12;
- Thunder and hail, 9:13–35;
- A plague of locusts, 10:1–20;
- Darkness, 10:21–29;
- Death of the first-born males of people and animals, 11:1–10, 12:29–32.

THE MIRACLE AT THE SEA (Exodus 13:17–14:31)

1 Although many questions might be asked about the Exodus ("Where did the people cross? How did God open a path through the water?"), the ancient Israelites did not concern themselves with these questions. What mattered to them was: In a moment of dire need, God rescued His people, prevented the Egyptians from making a direct attack on them, and finally destroyed their enemies, Exodus 14:30,31.

2 The Exodus event highlights the emphasis that the Old Testament places on God's control and use of water in creation and in the life of His people. In Genesis 1, God pushes back the waters to expose the surface of the earth. In Genesis 7, God calls back the waters to destroy the face of the earth, now wicked beyond redemption. In Genesis 8, God pushes those waters back into their place once again to begin Creation Two. In Exodus 14, God opens up a way through the sea to enable Israel to escape from Egypt. Later, God opens up the waters of the Jordan River to enable Israel to enter the Promised Land, Joshua 3.

7A When the Israelites first went into Egypt, they fared well and enjoyed a privileged position in the land. However, the day came when their situation changed dramatically. Freedom gave way to slavery.

7B The Israelites saw the exodus from Egypt as the most important event in their history. They celebrated the fact that the one who had rescued them from Egypt was the Creator of the universe. Not only had God rescued them from the power of the pharaoh, but He was now leading them to that land that He had long ago promised to Abraham and his descendants.

7C As the centuries and millennia passed by, the exodus from Egypt remained central to the thinking of the Israelites. When they thought about it, they did not merely recall it; they celebrated it as if all descendants of those who experienced it had themselves participated in it.

Eventually those who had been taken into exile in Babylon in 597 and 587 B.C. saw their rescue from Babylon as a second exodus event.

7D There is reason to believe that Joseph, and Jacob and his eleven other sons, settled in Egypt when foreign rulers, known as the Hyksos, ruled in Egypt. When the legitimate Egyptian rulers eventually drove out the Hyksos and regained control of Egypt, the pharaohs looked on the foreign Israelites with disdain and enslaved them.

Eventually a pharaoh, who knew nothing about the services Joseph had rendered to the Egyptians some centuries earlier, enslaved the Israelites and commanded midwives serving the Israelites to kill all first-born males.

To deal with the situation, God raised up Moses. Although Moses had risen to a position of power in Egypt, he was forced to flee after killing an Egyptian who was harassing an Israelite. God revealed His presence to Moses in the wilderness, and sent him and his brother Aaron to confront the Pharaoh.

7E The Egyptians believed that the pharaohs were more than mere mortals. They looked on them as embodiments of the deity, sons of the gods of Egypt, and believed that they possessed superhuman wisdom and power. However, the pharaoh whom Moses and Aaron confronted did not realize that they were representatives of the creator of the universe—the only God!

The pharaoh soon found himself on the receiving end of a series of plagues that devastated his land, its resources, and its population. The result was that the pharaoh finally agreed to permit the Israelites to leave Egypt. After the Israelites set out, the pharaoh changed his mind and sent his forces to deal with them.

When Israel's position appeared hopeless, God delivered the people in an awesome way and dealt a final, devastating blow to the pharaoh and his forces. God opened up the waters to enable His people to escape, and then used those same waters to drown the Egyptian forces. The Israelites then began the long trek to the land that God had promised them centuries before.

CROSS WAYS®

1 SECTION

UNITS 1-10

From Creation to the Transjordan

UNIT 8

The Covenant at Sinai

Covenant: The Key to Understanding God's Relationship with Humanity

HITTITE TREATY FORMS

Help from Archaeology

Down through the millennia, nations, rulers, groups, and individuals have made agreements or covenants with each other—and still do. Archaeologists have unearthed examples of these ancient covenants.

ILLUSTRATION 8A depicts two kinds of covenant forms discovered by archaeologists in 1931. These covenant forms, inscribed on stone tablets, were used long ago by an ancient people called the Hittites who lived in the region now known as Turkey. (Genesis 23 refers to Abraham buying a field and burial cave from Ephron the Hittite.)

Upper section

PARITY Treaty

The word parity indicates that **two rulers of equal rank** made this kind of treaty with one another. This treaty was an *agreement*, a *two-way affair*, because both parties discussed, and agreed to, its contents.

Lower section

SUZERAINTY or VASSAL Treaty

This treaty was made by a powerful king or *suzerain* (**large crowned figure**) with a less important ruler or *vassal* (**small crowned figure**). It was not an agreement. The suzerain drew it up, and imposed it on the vassal. The sequence of thoughts underlying this treaty was as follows:

❶ The *suzerain* introduced and described himself to the *vassal.*

❷ The suzerain listed his past acts of generosity and kindness toward the vassal (**scroll, three dots, arrow pointing to the past**).

❸ The suzerain told the vassal in detail how he, the vassal, was to live and act (**law-codes**).

In the ancient non-biblical world, these treaties or covenants were always made between *people or nations—* never between *a god and a nation*, or between *a god and a person*.

The Bible, however, refers to *God* making a covenant with *Israel* at Sinai—a covenant whose structure resembles that of a Hittite suzerainty treaty.

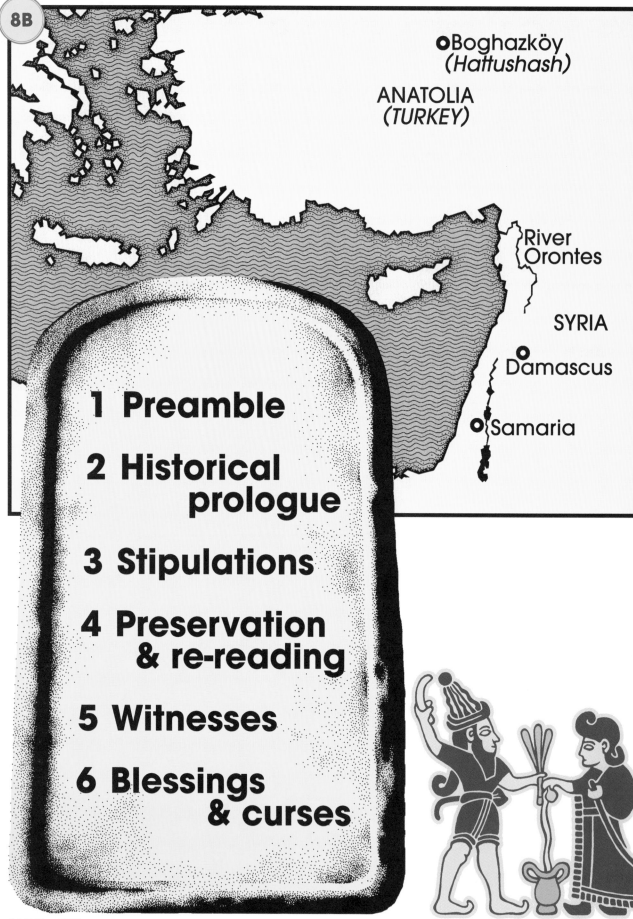

Boghazköy
(*Hattushash*)

ANATOLIA
(*TURKEY*)

River
Orontes

SYRIA

Damascus

Samaria

1 Preamble

**2 Historical
prologue**

3 Stipulations

**4 Preservation
& re-reading**

5 Witnesses

**6 Blessings
& curses**

© H. N. Wendt 2006

The Structure of a Hittite Treaty

A Hittite SUZERAINTY or VASSAL Treaty

The treaty patterns inscribed on tablets unearthed by archeologists in 1931 were found in the ruins of ancient *Boghazköy* near *Hattushash* in present-day *TURKEY* (whose ancient name was *ANATOLIA*). The treaty pattern usually contains six parts—although not every treaty discovered contains all six. What follows is a simplified version of a suzerainty treaty made by a Hittite king, Mursilis, with a vassal king named Duppi-Tessub, ruler of Amurru land (that is, the land of the Amorites—later, the Syrians).

1 Preamble

I am the great king Mursilis, the king of Hatti land, the valiant, the favorite of the storm-god, the great king, the king of Hatti land, the valiant.

2 Historical prologue

My forefathers and I have always treated you and your forefathers well. We have protected you, been loyal to you, treated you justly, and have done nothing to arouse your anger. When your father died, I did not desert you but put you on the throne in your father's place, and made sure that your next of kin would be obedient to you.

3 Stipulations

You have taken oaths toward me and my next of kin. Remain true to them. You shall pay me the same tribute your father paid. You are not to try to make private arrangements with other nations. My friends must also be your friends, and my enemies your enemies. When you hear of others plotting against me, you are to let me know. When my land is under attack, you must come to my aid. When fugitives from my land flee to your land, you must take them into custody and return them to me.

4 Preservation and Re-reading

A copy of this treaty has been deposited in the temple of Hatti land before the sun-goddess. Another copy has been placed in the temple of your land before Tessub. It is to be read to you at regular intervals.

5 Witnesses

We call upon the gods to assemble in our presence and to witness what is written in this treaty. (Two lists of gods are then given: first those of the Hittites, and then those of Amurru land.)

6 Blessings and Curses

If Duppi-Tessub does not honor the treaty and oath written in this treaty, may the gods destroy Duppi-Tessub together with his wife, his son, his grandson, his house, his land, and everything he owns. But if Duppi-Tessub honors the words of this treaty and the oaths that are inscribed on this tablet, may the gods of the oath protect him and his wife, his son, his grandson, his house, and his country.

Lower right

This image is based on a carved relief showing a Hittite king (*right*) pouring a libation before a storm-god (*left*).

8C

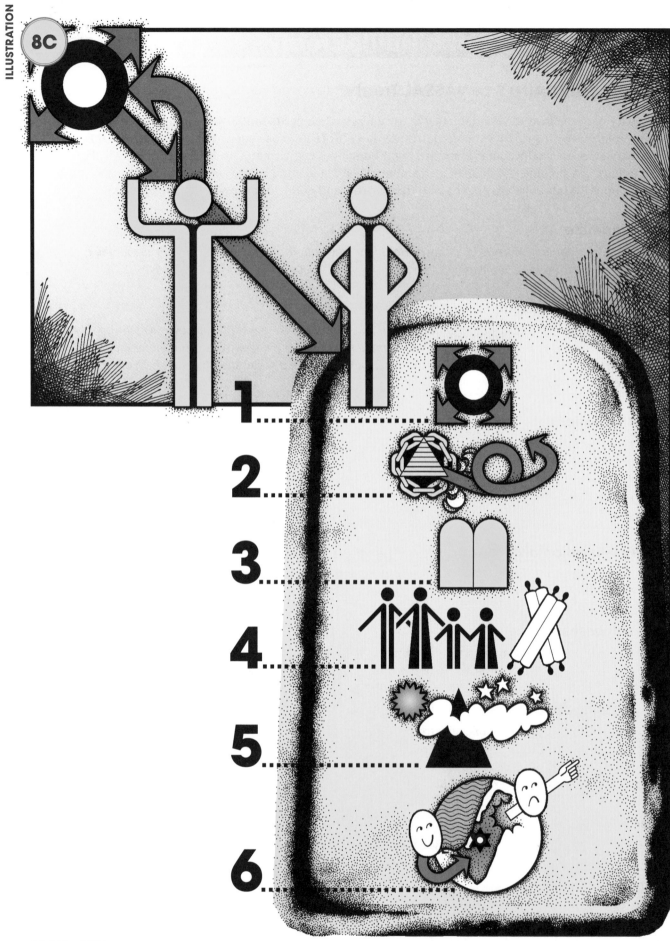

1 ....

2 ....

3 ....

4 ....

5 ....

6 ....

There are obvious similarities between the structure of Hittite Suzerainty or Vassal Treaties, and that of the Sinai Covenant. Admittedly, a complete example of a Covenant of Human Obligation cannot be found within the compass of a few verses in a single chapter in the Bible. However, portions of it occur so frequently in the Old Testament writings that one can only conclude that the Sinai Covenant parallels the Hittite form in spirit. To illustrate:

1 Preamble

God tells the people who God is: "I am the Lord your God," Exodus 20:2a (*symbol for God*).

2 Historical prologue

God tells the people what He has done for them: "...who brought you out of the land of Egypt, out of the house of slavery," Exodus 20:2b (*Egyptian pyramid, arrow through chains and water, circular arrow denoting journey through wilderness and entry into the Promised Land*).

3 Commandments (or Stipulations)

God tells the people what God expects them to do in response, Exodus 20:3–17. Exodus, Leviticus, Numbers, and Deuteronomy contain several collections of these commandments, or *law-codes*.

The people's obedience is not to be an attempt to *affect* (or, *bring about*) a relationship with God; the people's obedience is rather to *reflect* the relationship God has established with them. **The people are to serve one another as God has served them**, Deuteronomy 16:12 (top left).

4 Preservation and Re-reading

The covenant is to be written and stored (Exodus 31:18; Deuteronomy 4:13; 31:9, 24–26), read and taught to present and future generations of Israelites (Deuteronomy 6:6–9; 31:10–13), and obeyed (*parents with children, scrolls*).

5 Witnesses

Witnesses watch over the covenant to ensure that it is kept, Deuteronomy 4:26; 30:19; 31:28; Joshua 24:22, 27. In non-Israelite covenant forms, the gods are called on to serve as witnesses to the covenants which earthly kings made with each other. In Israel, the forces of nature (*sun, stars, mountain, cloud*) and the people themselves serve as witnesses to the covenant God made with His people.

6 Blessings and Curses

God tells the people that if they take God's covenant with them seriously, all will go well with them (*smiling face*) in Canaan (*arrow pointing to the Promised Land*), Deuteronomy 28:1–14. God also tells them that if they do not take the covenant seriously, things will go badly for them (*sad face*), Deuteronomy 27:15–26; Joshua 8:34. Not only that, but they will lose the land to a foreign power and be taken into exile (*hand pointing to a distant land*), Deuteronomy 28:15–68. See also Exodus 23:20–33; Leviticus 26.

BIBLICAL COVENANT FORMS

DIVINE COMMITMENT

HUMAN OBLIGATION

Abraham and Sinai Covenants Compared 8D

God took the initiative in making both covenants, and both flow from God's grace. However, it is important to understand how these two covenants differ from each other. **ILLUSTRATION 8D** depicts the differences.

Upper section

The Covenant with Abraham: DIVINE COMMITMENT

This was a *one-way* affair, from God to Abraham. Abraham contributed nothing; he merely received. In the covenant with Abraham, God formed a *people*.

It contained future promises (***yellow arrow pointing forward; scroll depicting God's promises of land, offspring, and blessings to the nations***).

From God's perspective, it was meant to be *permanent*. God remains faithful to His promises.

God made a similar covenant with David, 2 Samuel 7:1–17. In the covenant with David, God promised a *dynasty* (a line of kings) to rule over Abraham's descendants, the Israelites. Although the word "forever" is used a number of times in 2 Samuel 7, the Davidic line of kings came to an apparent end when King Jehoiachin and King Zedekiah were taken into exile in Babylon in 597 and 587 B.C., and eventually died there. The dynasty was restored in a radical manner when Jesus the Messiah, a descendant of David, was born in Bethlehem, Matthew 1:1.

A very important word shows up frequently with regard to the covenants with Abraham and David. That word is "*if*"; see 1 Kings 2:4; 9:4,6. God will remain true to His promises; however, *if the people worship other gods*, they will sever their relationship with the God of the patriarchs and the Exodus. They will lose the Promised Land, Jerusalem, the Temple, the Davidic dynasty, and their status as God's people, 1 Kings 9:1–9.

Lower section

The Covenant of Sinai: HUMAN OBLIGATION

❶ This covenant was a *two-way* affair. God *made* it; Israel was to *respond* to it.

❷ In this covenant, God made no future promises. God merely listed what He had done for the Israelites in the past (***yellow arrow pointing backward; scroll depicting the Exodus from Egypt, and God's promises of offspring and land***).

❸ It contained commandments (***law-codes***). The people were to respond to God's goodness by serving God and one another within the community (***arrows from each person to God and neighbor***).

Israel could always break the covenant God made with them at Sinai by *persistent disobedience*—by breaking the law-codes that were part and parcel of that covenant, Deuteronomy 8:11–20, 28:15–68.

An understanding of the similarities between the Hittite suzerainty treaty and the Sinai covenant form can prove helpful. In what follows, reference is made first to the Hittite form, and then to the biblical form.

 Preamble

The treaty is between a major power, the Hittites, and a subordinate kingdom, Amurru. Only the Hittite king is called "great." It is his treaty, not in the sense that he is expected to obey it, but in the sense that he granted it.

Biblical form:
The great Lord God of the universe says to little Israel, "This is who *I am*," Exodus 20:2.

 Historical prologue

The relationship between the Hittites and Amurru is outlined, going back a generation or two. Emphasis is placed on the kindness of the Hittite king, a factor designed to base the relationship between the two parties on something other than force.

Biblical form:
After rescuing the Israelites from Egypt, God says, "This is what *I have done for you*," Exodus 20:2.

Commandments (or **Stipulations**)

The Hittite king does not suggest that he is in any way under obligation to the vassal. He merely outlines his *past* actions on the vassal's behalf and assures him that his patronage will continue. The stipulations place the obligation to be loyal and obedient *on the vassal*.

Biblical form:
In giving the commandments, God says, "This is what *I expect of you* in response," Exodus 20:3–17.

Preservation and Re-reading

The treaty is placed in the chief shrine of each land so that the gods, aware of the oath sworn in their presence, can remind the parties involved to remember its contents. From time to time, it is to be read to the vassal king.

Biblical form:
God's will is: "Write, store, read, and heed the covenant." (See Deuteronomy 6:1–9.)

Witnesses

The overlord's gods are mentioned first; they are the most numerous and powerful. The gods of the vassal are mentioned second; they are fewer in number and less powerful. In some treaties, things of nature also served as witnesses.

Biblical form:
God says, "I see and know all that you do in relation to My covenant. Take it seriously."

 Blessings and curses

If the vassal takes the covenant seriously, things will go well with him. If he proves disobedient, he and all that is his will be destroyed.

Biblical form:
God says, "Your well-being depends on what you do with the covenant I made with you at Mt. Sinai. If you take it seriously, you will be blessed," Deuteronomy 28:1–14. "If you persist in breaking it, you will be cursed," Deuteronomy 28:15–68, Leviticus 26.

A ROYAL GRANT Treaty

The covenant with Abraham also has a prototype in the Ancient Near Eastern world—a prototype known as a *Royal Grant Treaty*. In this kind of treaty, someone with power and influence gives property or authority to a lesser person. The elements of the Royal Grant Treaty are similar to those found in the Sinai covenant. It usually contains an additional section, as defined in part seven below.

 Preamble

The donor introduces himself by name and title; see Genesis 15:7, 17:1.

 Historical prologue

The past relations of the donor and the recipient are described. The reasons for the grant being made are stated. Either the donor is rewarding the recipient for services rendered, or the donor wishes to further his own political agenda; see Genesis 15:6; 26:5.

 Stipulations

If the recipient is a privileged vassal, the stipulations are formulated in the vassal's interest, e.g., the gift is made to the vassal in perpetuity. If the recipient is a less important person, the stipulations are written to the advantage of the donor, e.g., the recipient will lose the gift if he betrays the donor; see Genesis 15:4,5; 17:8.

 Preservation and Re-reading

The details are similar to those in section four of a Hittite Suzerainty Treaty.

 Witnesses

The details are again similar to those in section five of a Hittite Suzerainty Treaty.

Blessings and curses

The interests of the recipient are protected. Any party who interferes with the recipient is declared cursed. The donor may even include a self-directed curse, to take effect if the donor violates the terms of the grant.

Specifications of the Granted Territory

The donor defines the boundaries of the grant; see Genesis 15:18–21; 17:8.

Making and Breaking Biblical Covenants 8G

1 Covenant, a Key Concept

The word "covenant" occurs frequently in the Bible. In addition to the covenants with Abraham and Israel, God made covenants with *Noah* (Genesis 9), *Phinehas* (Numbers 25:10–13), and *David*, 2 Samuel 7. Furthermore, the Genesis narrative speaks of both Abraham (21:27,32) and Isaac making covenants with *Abimelech*, 26:28.

2 The Covenant with Noah

The Covenant with Noah follows the creation and flood narratives, Genesis 9. God promises that never again will the "windows of the heavens" and the "fountains of the great deep" (Genesis 7:11) open to allow the cosmic waters to flood the habitable regions of the earth. The stage on which the ensuing divine drama is to be played out is secure.

3 Covenant Sealing Ceremonies

- The Hebrew term for making a covenant means literally "to cut a covenant"; see Jeremiah 34:18. Genesis 15:7–21 describes God—after making a solemn covenant promise to Abraham—passing between the halves of animals cut in two. (See 5C.)
- Isaac and Abimelech concluded a covenant agreement by sharing a meal together, Genesis 26:30.
- Other ceremonies were used in making and sealing a covenant. Both parties drank from a common cup, or made use of oil or water in rituals in which they either drank the water or smeared the oil on their skin. Possibly these rituals were enacted statements which declared: "If I break the covenant, may the curses enter my body as does this water (or oil)." See Psalm 109:18; Hosea 12:1; Jeremiah 2:18.

4 Covenant Ratification Ceremonies

The ceremony outlined in Exodus 24:1–8 appears to be a covenant ratification ceremony. An altar is built. Animals are sacrificed and some of their blood is sprinkled on the altar. Moses reads the book of the covenant to the people—who respond with a pledge of obedience. Moses then flings the remainder of the blood over the people. Apparently the ritual signified the uniting of the two parties involved in the covenant: God and the people. The use of blood reflected the view that blood (which is believed to contain life) is efficacious in establishing a relationship between God and humanity, Deuteronomy 27:5–8; Joshua 8:31–35; Mark 14:24; 1 Corinthians 11:25.

After the covenant ratification ceremony referred to in Exodus 24:1–8, Moses, Aaron, Aaron's two sons, and seventy elders go up the slopes of Sinai, see the God of Israel, and share a meal with Him, Exodus 24:9–11. Later, Moses experiences a *theophany* (symbols of God's heavenly presence), Exodus 24:15–18; see Luke 9:28–36.

5 Covenant Renewal Ceremonies

These played an important role in the life of the Israelites. Their purpose was to keep the faith alive and vital within the community, and to give each Israelite an opportunity to give personal assent to the covenant, Joshua 8:30–35; 24:1–28.

6 Covenant Reparation Ceremonies

The people held these when they became aware that they were guilty of some serious breach of the covenant, 2 Kings 23:1–3. Their purpose was to avert, if possible, the threatened and impending doom.

7 Covenant Confirmation Ceremonies

These were held in times of national crisis—for example, after the death of an important leader when power was transferred to a successor, 1 Samuel 12; 2 Kings 11:17–20; 2 Chronicles 23:16–21. Nehemiah 9 speaks of covenant observances in connection with a reform movement undertaken by exiles who returned from Babylon.

8 To Last—or Not to Last?

When God made a covenant with *Abraham*, He committed Himself to future actions on His people's behalf without imposing expectations and obligations on them. The covenant with Abraham gave the Israelites hope and confidence. No matter what Israel's condition, there was always reason for hope. Although the people had been unfaithful to God and had run after other gods, the hope remained that He would remember His initial promises and receive them back into fellowship with Himself.

9 Revocable

The covenant God made with Israel at Mt. Sinai was different in implication. It placed obligations on Israel. Failure to live up to it could have dire consequences. God would revoke the covenant, and the curses spelled out in the covenant structure would overwhelm the nation. *This conviction lay at the very core of the proclamations of the prophets.*

10 The Land

The book of Deuteronomy insists that the Promised Land was and remained the Lord's property. Behind this attitude lay a deep understanding of the significance of property and of the obligations associated with its use. Israel's sojourn in Canaan was not necessarily permanent. The Israelites were a tenant people and could lose the land if they persisted in breaking the Sinai covenant, Deuteronomy 4:25–28; 5:32,33; 11:13–17; 28:1–68. See also Leviticus 25:23,24; Jeremiah 2:7; Hosea 9:3.

8A During the past century, archaeologists have unearthed stone tablets on which are inscribed treaties between ancient rulers. They contain two forms:

- A covenant between equals—a *parity* treaty.
- A covenant between a powerful ruler and a lesser ruler—a *suzerainty* or *vassal* treaty.

8B A suzerainty or vassal treaty contained six parts:

- A *preamble*
- An *historical prologue*
- A list of *stipulations* or commandments
- Provisions for the *preservation and re-reading* of the covenant
- A list of divine *witnesses* to the treaty
- *Blessings and curses*—the implications of honoring or breaking the covenant

8C The covenant God made with the Israelites at Mt. Sinai had a structure similar to that of a suzerainty or vassal treaty. The stipulations in this covenant summoned Israel to do the will of God—not to *become* God's people (Israel already was that), but to *demonstrate gratitude to God* for His gracious action towards the nation. Although Israel was not saved *by works*, Israel was saved *for works*. Israel's life under God was to be an attempt to live the way He first intended humanity to live together under Him. It was to be an attempt to restore the harmony that had prevailed prior to humanity's first rebellion. Furthermore, Israel's obedience was to serve as a magnet to attract other nations and peoples into fellowship with God, so that they might join in praising and serving that one true God.

8D The covenant made with Abraham (and later, David) was a covenant of divine commitment—a covenant in which God listed the things that He would do for Abraham and his descendants. Although God would remain faithful to His promises, Abraham and his descendants could negate the covenant if they persisted in worshiping false gods.

The covenant God made with the Israelites at Mt. Sinai was a two-way affair. God made it. The Israelites were to respond to it by studying and obeying the commandments it contained. If they took the covenant seriously, they would be blessed. If they persisted in breaking God's commandments, God's curses would overtake them.

8E Research done by biblical scholars has helped Bible students understand the nature of the covenants referred to in the biblical materials and the role they play in the biblical narrative.

8F Recent research by biblical scholars suggests that there is a similarity between the covenant God made with Abraham and another ancient covenant form, a Royal Grant Treaty.

8G Genesis 9–11 refer to a covenant God made with Noah. The Old Testament writings contain numerous references to ceremonies relating to the sealing, ratification, renewal, reparation, and confirmation of a covenant.

CROSS WAYS

SECTION 1

UNITS 1–10

From Creation to the Transjordan

UNIT 9
The Law-Codes

God's Will for Creation and Humanity

Life In The Presence Of God

Exodus 19:1,2 refers to the Israelites arriving at Mt. Sinai; Numbers 10:11,12 refers to their departure from Mt. Sinai. The sixty chapters between these two passages focus on what took place during the period at Mt. Sinai. They contain a number of law-codes. Several more law-codes are given in the latter chapters of Numbers and in the book of Deuteronomy.

 ILLUSTRATION 9A shows the symbol for **Mt. Sinai**. At its summit are symbols of the presence of God among the people (*cloud*, *lightning*).

② On Mt. Sinai is the *symbol for the covenant God made with Israel at Sinai*. On it are *five black circles*, with a *symbol for law-codes at position 3*; these six details refer to the six parts of the Sinai covenant referred to in **ILLUSTRATION 8C**.

③ The illustration also shows the *community of Israel*, *with hands joined*, around Mt. Sinai. Although the covenant summoned each Israelite to a *personal faith*, it also summoned that person to a *community responsibility*. **Each person was to live to serve God by serving others.**

The Bible knows of no such thing as a *private* relationship with God. Either Christianity destroys the privacy, or the privacy destroys Christianity.

Personal faith, *yes*; *private* faith, *never*!

In today's world, those wishing to engage in a certain activity or pursue a certain lifestyle must ask, "If everyone were to do what I plan to do, or to live as I choose to live, what would happen to the human race?" If the answer is that it would harm or destroy the human race, no person has a right to perform that action or pursue that lifestyle. A Chinese proverb states, "When a butterfly flaps its wings in China, it affects the weather patterns around the planet."

④ The *Tabernacle* is depicted at the base of Mt. Sinai.

- Exodus 25–31 and 35–40 refer to the building of an elaborate Ark of the Covenant and Tabernacle. Numbers 2 locates the Tabernacle at the very center of the camp. Numbers 4:48 states that it was cared for by 8,580 Levites.

- Exodus 33:7–11 describes a much more simple structure, referred to as the Tent of Meeting. Deuteronomy 10:1–5 refers to Moses building a rather simple Ark out of acacia wood. The Tent of Meeting was located at some distance from the camp and cared for by one person—Joshua.

The narratives relating to the location of the Tabernacle/Tent of Meeting in the life of the Israelites after their entry into Canaan under Joshua lack clarity. Whatever the nature of these structures was, the Israelites understood themselves to be living in and around the presence of God, who was enthroned above the Ark of the Covenant within the Holy of Holies of the Tabernacle and, later, within the Holy of Holies of the Jerusalem Temple. See 1 Samuel 4:4; 2 Samuel 6:2; 2 Kings 19:15; 1 Chronicles 13:6.

⑤ The law-codes given at Sinai were to serve as:

a. *Guidelines for copying God.* At Sinai, God said, "This is how I have treated you; treat one another as I have treated you."

b. *Guidelines for living in community;* see point 3 above.

c. *Guidelines for witnessing.* Israel's obedience was to serve as a magnet to draw other nations into fellowship with God; see Deuteronomy 4:1–8, especially vv. 6–8.

d. *Guidelines for experiencing joy.* Obedience would create joy both in the life of the person who served, and in the life of the person being served, Psalm 119.

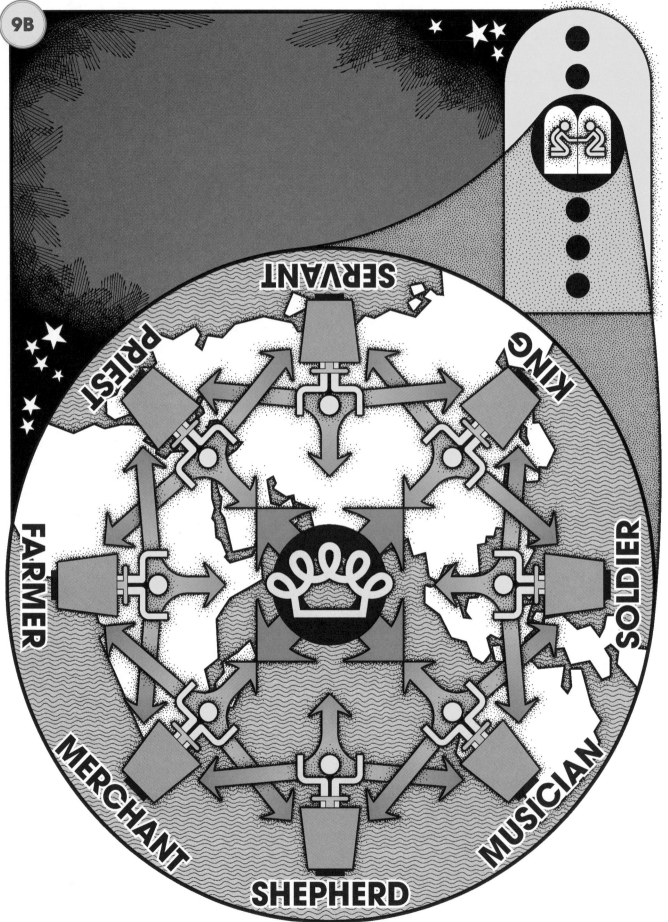

SERVANT

PRIEST

KING

FARMER

SOLDIER

MERCHANT

MUSICIAN

SHEPHERD

A Kingdom of Priests

THE PRIESTHOOD DEFINED

1 After God gathered the Israelites around His presence at Mt. Sinai, God said to them, "Indeed, the whole earth is mine, but you shall be for me a priestly kingdom and a holy nation," Exodus 19:5b,6. God then made a covenant with them, Exodus 20.

2 In referring to them as a *priestly kingdom*, God did not mean that they were to do nothing but perform rituals in the Tabernacle and Temple. Rather, they were to live under God as their *King*, and to serve Him as *priests* in all they did.

3 In this context, what is meant by the term *priest*? A priest is someone who:

    a.   Handles *sacred things*;

    b.   Goes *to God for others*, and *to others for God*.

4 What are *sacred things*? God says, "The whole earth is mine." Everything we touch has a *sacred quality*, for God *made* and *owns* all things.

5 All people are called to serve as God's priests full-time, in that they are called to glorify God and serve others in all they do. Christianity focuses on this call.

THE PRIESTHOOD DEMONSTRATED

1 **ILLUSTRATION 9B** depicts *Planet Earth* with the *symbol for God* superimposed on it. God is King (*crown*) of the creation He made and owns.

2 Around God are *eight green pulpits. A person stands in each pulpit with arms raised in praise.* Beneath each pulpit is a *term denoting a calling in life*. *All* God's people, no matter what their calling, stand on *holy ground* and are in a *sacred situation* before God.

3 In the *upper right-hand corner* is a *symbol for covenant; symbol for law-codes at position 3*. According to Jewish teachers, the 613 commandments listed in Exodus–Deuteronomy (the Ten Commandments plus an additional 603 commandments) were given exclusively to the Israelites and their descendants.

4 Throughout both the Old and New Testament periods, **the caring service God's people render to others is to serve as a magnet to draw others into a relationship with God**, Deuteronomy 4:1–8, especially vv. 6–8; John 13:34,35.

Although Leviticus 19:18 called the ancient Israelites to "love your neighbor as yourself," Jesus the Messiah went beyond that. He called—and calls—His followers to "love one another *as I have loved you*," John 13:34. **Jesus' servant life is the model for the godly life!**

Jesus, not other people, writes the agenda for our service of others. We do not serve others as *they* want us to serve them, nor do we serve others as *we* might want to serve them. We serve them as *Jesus the Messiah* wants us to serve them.

BECAUSE

THEREFORE

People do not earn acceptance from God by good deeds. They cannot! God never intended that people even try to do this. All such attempts are misguided and contrary to God's will, Romans 3:27,28. Throughout the Bible, God first tells people who He is and what He has done for them. Only then does God state what He wishes people to do for Him. They are to serve Him by serving others.

ILLUSTRATION 9C depicts the biblical sequence: "**BECAUSE** I (God)—**THEREFORE** you (humanity)."

Upper section

BECAUSE I, GOD

Left segment, **Exodus 1** (see **ILLUSTRATION 7A**; Deuteronomy 6:20–25, 15:15; Joshua 24:1–13). God rescued the Israelites from slavery in Egypt, and led them through the wilderness into the Promised Land.

In the Historical Prologue of the Old Testament covenant format, the Israelites listed God's mighty acts toward them. In Genesis–Joshua, these are five in number:

- The call of Abraham;
- The rescue from Egypt;
- The events at Sinai (sometimes omitted);
- The wilderness wanderings;
- The conquest of Canaan under Joshua.

In later Old Testament writings, *creation* and the *covenant with David* are added to the list. As Israel's history progressed, the people updated their list of God's continuing acts on the nation's behalf, Joshua 24:1–13; Nehemiah 9. They saw God's involvement with them not merely as ancient history, but as a relationship in which God continued to act on their behalf.

God emphasized that His choice of Israel had nothing to do with *numbers* or *righteousness*. Israel's numbers were *small* (Deuteronomy 7:7,8), and Israel's righteousness was *non-existent*, Deuteronomy 9:4–6. **The key word throughout the Bible is consistently *grace*.** The law-codes were not given so that Israel might try to *become* God's children by obeying them. They were given to a people who *already belonged to God*. They were not given to the Israelites to *establish* a relationship with God, but to serve as guidelines for *reflecting* the relationship God had already established with them.

Right segment, **Exodus 2**. The illustration contains symbols of:

a. Jesus' life (**Servant-King**)
b. Jesus' crucifixion (**cross**)—in reality, Jesus' coronation (**crown above cross**)
c. Jesus' resurrection (**open tomb**)
d. Jesus' ascension (**arrow rising into a cloud**)
e. The Holy Spirit (**dove**)

In the original Greek of Luke 9:31, the word translated as "departure" is *exodus*; the word translated in some English Bibles as "accomplish" would be better translated as *complete*. Jesus' ministry was a "rescue event" which rescued humanity from the dominion of the deadly trio of Satan, sin, and death.

Lower section

THEREFORE YOU, MY PEOPLE

This section depicts the desired human response to God's grace. God wants people to *serve one another in community* (**circle of small circles**, **two servant figures**).

Since the fall into sin, human nature wants to reverse God's order of *divine action* (**BECAUSE**) and *human response* (**THEREFORE**). People think, "*Because* I am doing all these good things for God, *therefore* God will do good things for me." They see the commandments as a *merit system* (*a means of earning God's favor*) rather than as a *response system* (guidelines for saying "thank you" to God for His mercy and goodness).

Some people think that there is really only one law code in the Old Testament: the Ten Commandments. However, even a quick glance through Exodus, Leviticus, Numbers, and Deuteronomy reveals that these books contain several collections of laws.

NATIONAL AND COMMUNITY LIFE

 The Ten Commandments (Exodus 20:2–17; Deuteronomy 5:6–21)**:** This collection sets forth the basic provisions of the Sinai Covenant. It stresses the importance of loyalty to God and forbids any attempt to make images of God. These points are basic to the Israelite faith.

- In Exodus, the people are to observe the Sabbath to remember that after God created the universe, God rested on the seventh day. In Deuteronomy, they are to observe the Sabbath to remember that God rescued them from Egypt.
- In Exodus, coveting a neighbor's house is mentioned first, and coveting a neighbor's wife second; in Deuteronomy, this order is reversed.

The Covenant Code (Exodus 20:22–23:19)**:** This collection of laws has a close relationship with the Sinai Covenant and takes its name from Exodus 24:7. Many of its details apply to situations and conditions within Canaan, e.g., 22:5,6.

The Ritual Decalogue (Exodus 34:10–26)**:** This collection of laws is given in a context where one expects the Ten Commandments to be given a second time. (Exodus 32 reports the incident of the golden calf and Moses smashing the first set of law tablets; note 32:21–24!) Although the code is intended to replace the original Ten Commandments, it deals instead with ritual details. In 34:1, God says He Himself will write the commandments; in 34:27, God tells Moses to write them. Exodus 34:6,7 contains a preamble that is rich in grace, but nevertheless calls the people to responsible obedience. Exodus 34:29–35 describes the effect that being in God's presence had on Moses' appearance.

 The Deuteronomic Code (Deuteronomy 12–26)**:** The setting in Deuteronomy is the east bank of the Jordan River. Israel is poised to cross into Canaan. In Deuteronomy, Moses gives the people a final and lengthy exhortation, urging them to dedicate their lives totally to serving the God of Israel and to serve Him at a single (unnamed) sanctuary. Deuteronomy contains detailed "blessing and curse" passages, 27:15–26; 28:1–68. If the people serve God faithfully, they will live long in the land and prosper. If they forsake God and worship other gods, a host of curses will overtake them, and they will lose the land and go into exile.

NATIONAL WORSHIP LIFE

 The Priestly Code: This is not a single, compact collection of laws. It is a series of collections scattered throughout Numbers and Leviticus. It deals with matters of religious ritual and serves to amplify and integrate the other codes. Some of the more significant subjects it deals with are:

Numbers 28,29......Festivals
Leviticus 1–7......Offering of sacrifices
8–10......Priesthood
11–15......Distinction between clean and unclean
16......Day of atonement

The Holiness Code (Leviticus 17–26)**:** This code gets its name from its contents and from the refrain that occurs repeatedly within it: "Be holy, for I, the Lord your God, am holy." It deals with subjects such as the ritual slaughter of animals, sexual relations, the regulation of daily life within the community, the special status of priests, annual feasts, the sabbatical year, the year of jubilee, vows, and tithes.

TYPES OF LAWS

Several different kinds of laws can be discerned. These are:

1 **Command:** "You shall not revile God," Exodus 22:28.

2 **Statute:** "When a slave-owner strikes a male or female slave with a rod and the slave dies immediately, the owner shall be punished," Exodus 21:20.

3 **Statute with exhortation:** "When you reap your harvest in your field and forget a sheaf in the field, you shall not go back to get it; it shall be left for the alien, the orphan, and the widow, so that the Lord your God may bless you in all your undertakings," Deuteronomy 24:19.

4 **Cultic Ordinance:** "If any one of you sins without knowing it... you shall bring to the priest a ram without blemish from the flock, or the equivalent, as a guilt offering; and the priest shall make atonement on your behalf for the error that you committed unintentionally, and you shall be forgiven," Leviticus 5:17,18.

PRINCIPLES WITHIN THE LAW-CODES

1 Central to Israel's understanding of God's relationship with the nation was that God had *chosen* Israel. Israel belonged uniquely to God. However, Israel had not been chosen merely for *privilege*—although privilege was involved. Israel had been chosen also for *responsibility*, to be subject to divinely imposed obligations, Deuteronomy 27:9,10. Remembering God's goodness and obedience to God were to go hand in hand. Obedience was to lie at the very heart and center of Israel's life, Deuteronomy 32:46,47.

2 Because Israel was God's *elect* people, Israel was also to be *unique* among the nations. Israel was to be *holy*, or *set apart*. God was holy because God was supremely *different*. Israel was therefore to be like God, Leviticus 19:2. This being *unique*, *different*, *set apart*, and *holy* was to demonstrate itself in several ways:

    a. An Israelite was to practice a certain *exclusiveness* in relation to other nations. No covenants were to be made with them, Exodus 23:32; 34:12–16. No intermarriage was allowed, Exodus 34:16; Deuteronomy 7:3. Any action that would blemish the people of God was forbidden. Those who cut themselves off from the people of God and became apostate were to be destroyed, Deuteronomy 13:12–18; 17:2–7.

    b. Because the Israelites were God's special people, they were to be different from the people of other nations in terms of what they ate and wore. The significance of some of the Pentateuch's details concerning these requirements are somewhat puzzling. At times, that which seems to matter a lot is placed side by side with that which seems to matter only a little. To illustrate, Leviticus 19:17–19 begins by laying down the greatest of ethical principles, "love your neighbor as yourself," and concludes with a command not to wear clothing made by blending different materials. It is possible that eventually the Israelites themselves forgot the origin and significance of these details, and observed them for their own sake. (See Exodus 34:26, "You shall not boil a kid in its mother's milk." Some suggest it has links to Canaanite religious practices; others see it as a commandment given to encourage compassion for the animal world. It eventually gave rise to the practice of equipping some Jewish kitchens with two different sets of cooking utensils, one for milk products and another for meat products.) With the passing of time, some within Israel focused on being different *just to be different*, with little awareness of the call to live to serve others.

At first glance, some Old Testament law-codes are puzzling. Deuteronomy 23:17,18 states:

> *None of the daughters of Israel shall be a temple prostitute; none of the sons of Israel shall be a temple prostitute. You shall not bring the fee of a prostitute or the wages of a male prostitute into the house of the Lord your God in payment for any vow, for both are abhorrent to the Lord your God.*

Why such a commandment? In Gentile nations, sacred prostitutes were often associated with temples. Profits from their trade were used to build additional temples. People did not object to this, because they made little connection between morality and religion.

A careful reading of the law-codes reveals their comprehensive character:

a. The law-codes were meant for every person in the community of Israel. The practice of "religion" was not something to be left to the "experts," or the "full-time professionals." Religion was what life itself was to be all about for each and every Israelite. (There is no Hebrew word for *secular.*)

b. The law-codes permitted no compartmentalization of life. The practice of religion was not to be thought of as a *part* of life, not even as the *most important part of life.* Life under God was to embrace *all* of life.

c. The law-codes spell out guidelines for behavior in a wide range of situations. The basic principles that underlie them are love of God and love of neighbor. A person serves God by serving others in the community.

d. The keeping of the law was not seen as a burden that took the fun out of life. For the Israelites, obedience to the law brought order and structure to life. The law is a precious gift of a gracious God. Psalm 119 sings its praises throughout its 176 verses.

e. The law-codes were to serve as guidelines to equip people to live together as God first intended humanity to live together—in caring, servant community.

SIGNIFICANT DETAILS OF THE LAW-CODES

Family life: Within the family, parents were to be honored, Exodus 20:12. To strike a parent was to merit the death penalty, Exodus 21:15; Deuteronomy 21:18–21. Due respect was to be paid to the aged, Leviticus 19:32. A newly-married man was to be given no business to do and was to be exempt from military service for one year, so as to be free and happy with his wife, Deuteronomy 20:5–7; 24:5.

The disadvantaged: Special consideration was to be given to the protection of widows and orphans, and the needy; they were held to be especially dear to God, Deuteronomy 1:17; 10:18; 16:19; Leviticus 19:15.

The poor: If ever a person found it necessary to offer an outer cloak as collateral for a loan, the pawn-broker had to give it back each night so that even in their poverty people could be warm when they slept, Exodus 22:26,27; Deuteronomy 24:10–13. No one was to accept a millstone as a pledge for a debt; the economic survival of the poor was at stake, Deuteronomy 24:6. A field of grain, grapes, or olives was not to be totally stripped at harvest time; something was always to be left for the poor and the stranger, Leviticus 19:9,10; Deuteronomy 24:20–22.

 Jew/Gentile: There was to be one set of laws for everyone, for both the *Jews* and the *aliens* (Gentiles) residing in their midst, Leviticus 24:22. At the same time, a Gentile could eat something forbidden a Jew (Deuteronomy 14:21), and Jews could demand something of a Gentile they could not demand of a fellow Jew, Deuteronomy 15:3; 23:19,20.

5 **Business ethics:** Business morality mattered greatly. The Pentateuch states seven times the need to have accurate weights and measures, e.g., Leviticus 19:35. God was concerned not just with what went on in the Temple and shrines, but also with what went on at the business counters and cash registers in the shops.

The wage paid for a day's work was a pittance. People could not get fat on it or save for the future. Therefore, employers had to pay their employees at the close of each day, Leviticus 19:13; Deuteronomy 24:14,15. The workers' survival depended on it.

6 **Moral responsibility:** People were responsible for their actions. They were accountable for the harm they did and for the harm they could have prevented, Exodus 21:28–32; Deuteronomy 22:8.

7 **The handicapped:** Deference was to be paid to the handicapped. A deaf man was never to be cursed, and a blind man was never to be tripped up, Leviticus 19:14; Deuteronomy 27:18.

8 **Concern for the animal world:** A lost ox or ass was to be returned to its owner or kept until claimed. An animal that had collapsed was to be helped to its feet again, Exodus 23:4,5; Deuteronomy 22:1–4. If a nest had to be robbed for the sake of food for the needy, the mother bird was always to be spared, Deuteronomy 22:6,7.

9 **Concern for nature:** If, in a time of war, wood was needed to construct siege barriers, fruit trees were not to be used for this purpose, Deuteronomy 20:19,20.

10 **Establishing integrity:** Very practical tests were to be used to determine the validity of a rape charge (Deuteronomy 22:23–27) and the worth of a prophet's prediction, Deuteronomy 18:20–22.

11 **Parental responsibility:** The responsibility for teaching children spiritual and moral truths was placed at the feet of parents, Deuteronomy 6:6,7; Joshua 4:19–24; Proverbs 22:6.

WHEN WERE THE LAW-CODES WRITTEN?

Two views prevail:

1 Some believe that God gave all law-codes to Moses at Sinai and on the plains of Moab. Those details which applied to life in the land of Canaan were given predictively to cover future needs and situations.

2 Some believe that although much of the legal material in the Pentateuch can be traced back to Moses, some of the details were added to meet new situations, e.g., Deuteronomy 17:14–20; note the commentary on this passage in 1 Samuel 8:10–18. Joshua wrote statutes and ordinances into the book of the law, Joshua 24:25,26. Samuel wrote guidelines for the rights and duties of a king into a book stored in the sanctuary, 1 Samuel 10:25.

9A After the exodus, when God gathered the Israelites around His awesome presence at Mt. Sinai, He first told them who He was and what He had done for them—and only then did He spell out how He wanted them to live. Obedience to the commandments was never to be seen as a way to *establish* a relationship with God. Rather, obedience to the commandments was to be seen as a way to *reflect* the relationship God had already established with His people. The law-codes were to serve as guidelines for:

- reflecting God's will;
- living in community;
- witnessing;
- experiencing joy.

9B God's people are to see all of life as a "sacred affair"—they live on a planet that God made and owns. Each dwells within a body God made and owns. In whatever they do, they are to see themselves as going to God for others, and then to others for God. There is no such thing as a secular realm.

9C Throughout the biblical narrative, God first tells His people who He is and what He has done for them—and only then does He tell them how they are to live under His Lordship. The sequence is always:

- *Indicative:* "Because I, God, have done this for you…
- *Imperative:* …therefore, this is how you are to think, speak, and act as My people."

9D Exodus–Deuteronomy contain six collections of law-codes:

- The Ten Commandments
- The Covenant Code
- The Ritual Decalogue
- The Deuteronomic Code
- The Priestly Code
- The Holiness Code

9E Different kinds of laws are found within these collections:

- Commands
- Statutes
- Statutes followed by an exhortation
- Ordinances that relate to rituals

Because the Israelites were to understand themselves as God's unique, holy, Chosen People, they were to act in a unique, holy manner in all that they did.

- They were to practice a certain *exclusiveness* in their dealings with other nations— in relation to things such as marriage and agreements.
- They were to be *different* in a variety of ways—e.g., in terms of what they wore and ate.

Life in relation to God was not merely something of Sabbath worship and ritual. It was something that applied to the totality of life:

- within the family circle;
- in business dealings;
- when dealing with the disadvantaged, the poor, Gentiles, the handicapped, the animal world, and the realm of nature.

Although some scholars and students believe that God gave all the law-codes in Exodus, Leviticus, Numbers, and Deuteronomy to Moses at Mt. Sinai, others believe that some of the law-codes contained in these writings were developed over a period of time and adapted to deal with new situations.

CROSS WAYS

1
SECTION

UNITS 1–10

From Creation to the Transjordan

UNIT 10
The Wilderness Wanderings

Events on the Way to the Promised Land

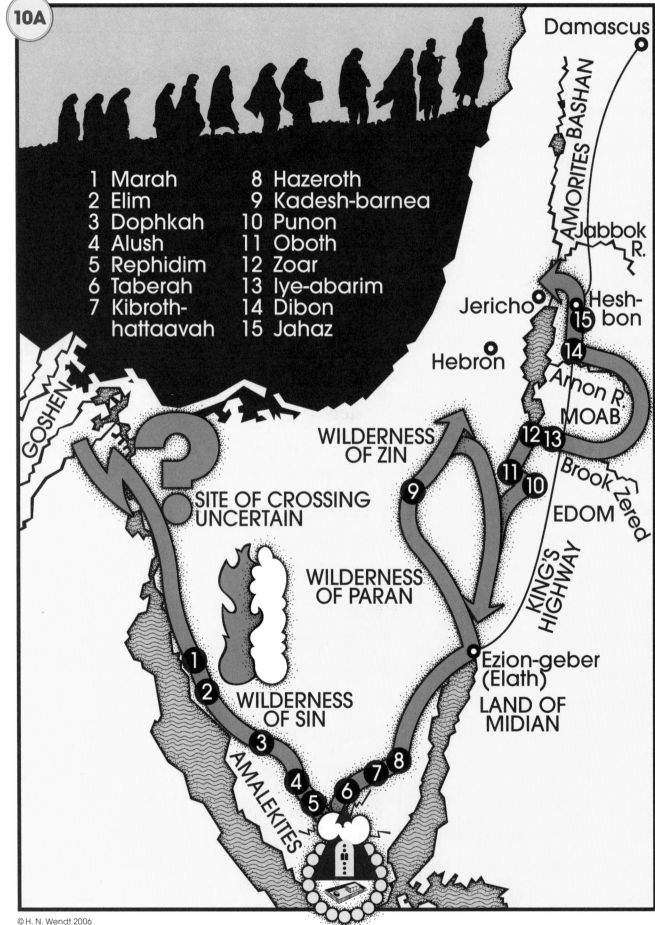

1 Marah
2 Elim
3 Dophkah
4 Alush
5 Rephidim
6 Taberah
7 Kibroth-hattaavah
8 Hazeroth
9 Kadesh-barnea
10 Punon
11 Oboth
12 Zoar
13 Iye-abarim
14 Dibon
15 Jahaz

Damascus

AMORITES BASHAN

Jabbok R.

Jericho

Hesh-bon

Hebron

Arnon R.

MOAB

WILDERNESS OF ZIN

Brook Zered

SITE OF CROSSING UNCERTAIN

EDOM

WILDERNESS OF PARAN

KING'S HIGHWAY

Ezion-geber (Elath)

WILDERNESS OF SIN

LAND OF MIDIAN

GOSHEN

AMALEKITES

© H. N. Wendt 2006

ILLUSTRATION 10A shows the *Israelites wandering through the wilderness* (*top left*) on their way to the *Promised Land*.

It is difficult to identify with any certainty some of the locations referred to in the narratives in Exodus, Numbers, and Deuteronomy that deal with the period of the wilderness wanderings. Some suggest, for example, that Mt. Sinai was located in the land of Midian to the east of the Gulf of Aqaba. On the Sinai Peninsula (a triangular land mass about 230 miles (370 kilometers) long and 150 miles (240 kilometers) wide at its northern end) is a depiction of the *route* many believe the Israelites followed.

Prior to leaving Egypt, the Israelites lived in **GOSHEN** in the Nile Delta, Exodus 9:26. After the Hyksos rulers were expelled from Egypt in about 1550 B.C., and the Egyptian pharaohs regained control, the Hebrews would have been looked on as despised pastoralists living among other "wretched Asiatics" and "sand dwellers"—terms the Egyptians used to refer to nomads who moved in and out of the Nile Delta. The Egyptians pressed foreigners into labor gangs, and forced them to serve as fieldhands and makers of bricks and mortar for the pharaoh's building projects.

When the 19th Egyptian dynasty came to power about 1306 B.C., the Pharaohs began to build treasure and storage cities—Pithom and Rameses—in the eastern part of the Nile Delta, the land of Goshen. After the tenth and final plague took its toll, the pharaoh commanded the Israelites to leave Egypt. Prior to leaving, the Israelites plundered the Egyptians of their jewelry, gold, silver, and clothing, 12:33–36. The Israelites traveled first from *Rameses* to *Succoth*, Exodus 12:37. A "mixed crowd" went with them (12:38), consisting most likely of other nomadic groups; see also Numbers 11:4.

Prior to leaving Egypt, the Israelites celebrated the passover (Exodus 12:43–13:10) and instructions were given about the consecration of the first-born, 13:1,11–16.

Just where they passed through the waters God opened to make possible their escape from Egypt is not known (**question mark**). God led them by means of a **pillar of cloud** by day and a **pillar of fire** by night, Exodus 13:17–22. References to the "Red Sea" in the biblical text should be translated as the "Reed Sea," referring to the marshy regions between the Gulf of Suez and the Mediterranean Sea.

Exodus 3:17 states that the Israelites did not travel up the eastern shore of the Mediterranean Sea "by way of the land of the Philistines," Exodus 13:17. Most likely they avoided it because of the many Egyptian fortresses along the military road linking Egypt to Canaan. *Migdol* and *Baal-Zephon* (Exodus 14:2, Numbers 33:7) are known from Egyptian sources as fortresses at the northeastern edge of the Nile Delta.

Although opinions differ concerning the actual route of the wilderness wanderings, the traditional view is that, after passing through the Reed Sea, the fugitives fled in a southeasterly direction toward the **WILDERNESS OF SIN**.

The **numbers** on the suggested route and **place names** (*upper left*) refer to but a few of the locations the Israelites encountered during this journey.

❶ After three days, they arrived at the oasis of **Marah**—which means "bitter"; the water there proved unfit for drinking. According to Exodus 15:22–26, Moses made the water sweet, and the people and their flocks were able to quench their thirst.

❷ They then moved on to **Elim** where they camped among its abundant springs and shady groves, Exodus 15:22.

However, as they began traveling through the **WILDERNESS OF SIN** water became more scarce and food began to run out. Some remembered the days in Egypt—days which now looked good to them compared with their miserable present and uncertain future. God came to the rescue of His grumbling people by providing them with manna, Exodus 16:1–36.

3 Numbers 33:12 states that **Dophkah** was the Israelites' first stopping place after they left the Wilderness of Sin.

4 From Dophkah, they moved on to **Alush** and set up camp, Numbers 33:13.

5 The next stopping place was **Rephidim**, Numbers 13:14—where, again, water was in short supply. After Moses struck a rock, the water problem was solved, Exodus 17:1–7.

While the Israelites were at Rephidim, Amalek and his followers attacked them, Exodus 17:8–16. Moses commissioned Joshua (his first mention in the Bible) to assemble soldiers to deal with the threat. While the battle took place, Moses held up his arms (eventually with help from Aaron and Hur) to ensure victory for the Israelites. Throughout their history, the Israelites continued to see the *Amalekites* as a thorn in the flesh, Deuteronomy 25:17–19; 1 Samuel 27:8–12. Haman the Agagite, referred to in Esther 3:1, was most likely an Amalekite; see also 1 Samuel 15:1–33.

Exodus 18 describes a meeting between Moses and his father-in-law, Jethro. Jethro shared a sacred meal with Moses and counseled him about the administration of law. Although Exodus 18:5 refers to the meeting taking place in the vicinity of Mt. Sinai, the narrative has not as yet made any reference to the Israelites arriving at Mt. Sinai. Numbers 10:29–32 refers to another conversation between Moses and Jethro—now called Hobab. (Exodus 2:18–22 states that Moses' father-in-law was Reuel; Numbers 10:29 states that Reuel was Hobab's father.)

Sinai *The arrival of the Israelites at Mt. Sinai is reported in Exodus 19:1. Their departure is described in Numbers 10:11. The events which took place at Mount Sinai are outlined in Units 7 and 8.*

Mt. Sinai is traditionally linked with Jebel Musa, or "Mountain of Moses." Located in the southern end of the Sinai peninsula, this red granite peak is about 7,500 feet (2,285 meters) high, and today has a chapel on its summit. It is not the highest peak in the region. Jebel Musa was associated with Mt. Sinai only in the 4th century A.D. when the Emperor Constantine's mother, Saint Helena, is said to have built a chapel and tower at the foot of the mountain to commemorate the place where, according to tradition, Moses saw the burning bush.

Emperor Justinian (A.D. 527–565) recognized Jebel Musa as a holy place by building a fortress monastery to protect the monks of his new church dedicated to the Virgin Mary. It was rededicated to Saint Catherine about the 10th century when relics of martyred saints were placed within it. According to 1 Kings 19, after his confrontation with the priests of Baal on Mt. Carmel, Elijah fled to a mountain south of Beer-sheba. The mountain is referred to as Horeb—the name that Deuteronomy uses for Mt. Sinai; see Exodus 3:1, 17:6, 33:6; Deuteronomy 1:2,6,19, 5:2; 1 Kings 8:9. The Koran (Islam's Holy Book) links Mount Sinai with Jebel Musa.

According to Exodus 32, while Moses speaks with the Lord on **Mt. Sinai**, the people persuade Aaron to make them some visible "gods," Exodus 32. When Moses comes down from the mountain and sees what is happening, he smashes the law tablets God has given him (Exodus 31:18, 32:19), burns the golden calf, grinds it to powder, mixes it with water, and makes the people drink the resulting mixture, 32:20.

When Moses confronts Aaron about why he made the golden calf, Aaron responds that the people forced him to do so. Aaron then states that after the people, at his command, gave him whatever gold they possessed, he threw it into a fire and the golden calf walked out from the flames, Exodus 32:21–24. Moses then commands the Levites to carry out a massive slaughter among the Israelites, Exodus 32:25–29. After the Levites do so, Moses tells them that they have ordained themselves

for the service of the Lord and have brought blessing on themselves, 32:28,29. Although the Lord threatens to withdraw His presence from Israel (32:30–35), He eventually relents—and mercy prevails.

Exodus 25–31 and 35–40 describe the building of an ornate Ark of the Covenant and an elaborate **Tabernacle**. It was located at the center of the camp and cared for by 8,580 Levites, Numbers 4:48. Exodus 33:7–11 speaks of Moses setting up a simple Tent of Meeting outside the camp; it was cared for by Joshua. Deuteronomy 10:1–5 speaks of Moses making a box in which he placed the law tablets God had given him.

In the spring—one year after escaping from Egypt—the Israelites left Mt. Sinai and headed for the **WILDERNESS OF PARAN**.

❻ The people's murmurings at **Taberah** provoked God to anger, Numbers 11:1–33. He destroyed part of their camp by sending fire among them. (*Taberah* means "burning.") In Deuteronomy 9:22, Taberah is linked with Massah and Kibroth-hattaavah as places where the Israelites provoked the Lord to wrath. It is not referred to in the itinerary outlined in Numbers 33.

❼ Numbers 30:35 links **Kibroth-hattaavah** ("graves of craving") to Taberah. Those who died because of their craving were buried there.

❽ **Hazeroth** ("enclosure," "settlement") is referred to in Numbers 11:35, 12:16, 33:17,18, and Deuteronomy 1:1. At Hazeroth, Aaron and Miriam had a dispute with Moses concerning his marriage with a Cushite woman and his unique position as the *sole* mediator between God and His people, Numbers 12:2. One of the outcomes was that Miriam found herself smitten with leprosy for seven days, Numbers 12:10–16.

Numbers 10:12 refers to the Israelites reaching the **WILDERNESS OF PARAN**. Numbers 33:35 says that **Ezion-geber** was one of their stopping-places.

❾ Eventually the Israelite community encamped at **Kadesh-barnea**, Numbers 13; see 13:26. The area around Kadesh-barnea was capable of supporting a large group of nomads for a long period of time. From there Moses sent twelve spies to survey the land of Canaan, Numbers 13:17. Each came from a different tribe, with Caleb from Judah and Joshua from the tribe of Ephraim (the latter's name was changed from Hoshea son of Nun to Joshua during this venture, 13:8,16).

The exploration group penetrated as far north as **Hebron**. After forty days, the spies returned with a glowing account of the land. (They brought back with them a cluster of grapes so heavy that it had to be carried on a pole between two men, Numbers 13:23,24. The Wadi Eshcol in the vicinity of Hebron is still today a famous grape-producing area.) However, they gave a gloomy report about the prospects of capturing it. They said that those who lived in the land were so huge that they themselves felt like grasshoppers, Numbers 13:33; see also Genesis 6:1–4. Although it was a land flowing with milk and honey, those who lived in it were strong and their cities were well fortified, Numbers 13:27–33. The spies who gave a negative report were afflicted by a plague and died, 14:36,37. Caleb, who gave a positive report, was spared (13:30), as was Joshua, 14:1–10.

Numbers 13:21 suggests that the spies went as far north as Rehob (2 Samuel 10:6), near Laish or Dan—to the north of the Sea of Galilee. Numbers 34:1–9 states that the boundaries of the Promised Land were to extend from the Wadi of Egypt (34:5) to Lebo-hamath (34:8), near Riblah on the Orontes River in Syria. These borders were established during the reign of David, 2 Samuel 8:3–14—the "star" who arose out of Jacob, Numbers 24:17–19.

After the spies returned, a half-hearted attempt was made to capture Canaan, but it failed miserably, Numbers 14:39–45. The people were told that they would have to wander in the wilderness for forty

years—one year for each day the spies were away, Numbers 14:34. No one who was more than twenty years of age would enter the Promised Land—with the exception of Joshua and Caleb, Numbers 14:20–24,29.

While the Israelites were at Kadesh-barnea, they experienced another water supply problem and murmured to Moses and Aaron. When Moses and Aaron prayed to God about the situation, God told Moses to command a rock to "yield its water," Numbers 20:1–8. Apparently Moses was told to use merely *words* to command the rock to produce. However, he *struck it with his rod.* Although an abundant supply of water flowed forth from the rock, Moses and Aaron were told that they would not enter the Promised Land because they had not trusted God. They had relied on Moses' *staff* to produce the water rather than on the *words* God wanted them to speak, 20:9–14.

During the time the Israelites were encamped at Kadesh-barnea, Miriam, the sister of Moses and Aaron, died, Numbers 20:1. A man who broke Sabbath laws was stoned to death, 15:32–36. When four priests (with 250 supporters) questioned the authority of Moses, the ground split apart and swallowed the priests and their families. Fire then came down from heaven and consumed the 250 supporters, Numbers 16:1–35. Moses then declared that only Aaron's descendants had authority to burn incense to the Lord, Numbers 16:36–40. The next day all of the Israelites rebelled against Moses and Aaron, and a plague broke out, which resulted in the deaths of 14,700 persons, Numbers 16:41–50. Numbers 27 describes how divine approval was given to Aaron and his descendants when Aaron's rod sprouted and produced blossoms and almonds, Numbers 17.

⑩ Many questions are raised concerning the route the Israelites followed to get from Kadesh-barnea to the plains of Moab north of the Dead Sea. Two different routes are given in Numbers, and the story is repeated with some variations in Deuteronomy. Numbers 33:35,36 and Deuteronomy 2:8 refer to them spending time at Ezion-geber. Numbers 33:42,43 states that they camped at **Punon**. Some scholars suggest that at times the Israelites traveled in groups, and that not all followed the same route. The following comments relate to the traditional route.

- From Kadesh-barnea, Moses sent envoys to the king of **EDOM** to request permission for the Israelites to pass through his territory. The envoys assured the Edomite king that the travelers would stay on the **KING'S HIGHWAY**—a busy trade route running from **Ezion-geber** in the south to **Damascus** in the north that passed through the hill country to the east of the Jordan valley. Permission was refused, Numbers 20:14–21.

- The Israelites were then compelled to make plans to travel around the eastern border of Edom, Numbers 21:4. Soon after setting out, they came to the vicinity of Mt. Hor—a few miles to the northeast of Kadesh-barnea. Aaron died there. Prior to his brother's death, Moses transferred Aaron's priestly garments to his son, Eleazar, Numbers 20:22–29.

- Numbers 21:1–3 refers to the Israelites slaughtering Canaanites and destroying their towns in the Negeb. The victors named the region Hormah ("destruction"). It is possible that this narrative is a parallel to that in Numbers 14:39–45.

- Soon afterwards, the Israelites complained once again about the lack of food and water. God responded by sending poisonous serpents among them, with the result that many died from snake-bites. God then told Moses to make a serpent and set it on a pole. Any person suffering from a snake bite who looked at what Moses had made was healed, Numbers 21:4–9. (See 2 Kings 18:4 and John 3:14,15.)

⑪ Numbers 33:43 reports that the Israelites camped at **Oboth** (actual site uncertain).

⑫ From the summit of Mount Nebo, God showed Moses the Promised Land extending as far southward as **Zoar**, Deuteronomy 34:3. Lot's older daughter bore him a son at Zoar, Genesis 19:37. The son's name was Moab; he became the father of the Moabites.

⑬ From Oboth, the people traveled to **Iye-abarim**—just to the south of the **Brook Zered**, Numbers 21:10–12.

⑭ After traveling around the eastern border of Edom, they set up camp "on the other side of the Arnon (River)," on the northern boundary of **MOAB**, Numbers 21:13. The **Arnon River** flows down a spectacular canyon 2½ miles (4 kilometers) wide.

Dibon, a city to the east of the Dead Sea and to the north of the Arnon River, was originally part of Moab. It was captured by Sihon, king of the Amorites—but taken from him by the Israelites, Numbers 21:23–30, 32:3. Eventually Moses gave the territory east of the Jordan River (including Dibon and other cities) to the tribes of Gad and Reuben, Numbers 32:33–42; see v. 34.

⑮ The Israelites then sought permission from Sihon, king of the **AMORITES** (whose capital was **Heshbon**), to use the King's Highway. Again permission was refused. This time the reaction of the Israelites to the refusal was different. They launched an attack on Sihon's territory and occupied the land from the **Arnon River** to the **Jabbok River**, Numbers 21:21–32.

After settling in Heshbon and its dependent villages, the people undertook another campaign in which they killed Og, king of Bashan, his sons, and all his people (including women and children, Deuteronomy 3:6), and took possession of his territory, Numbers 21:33–35. According to Deuteronomy 3:1–6, they captured sixty fortified cities with high walls, gates and bars, and a number of villages. However, they kept all the livestock in the region as spoil and booty, Deuteronomy 3:7. Deuteronomy 2:10,11 and 3:11 suggest that Og was a giant.

The Israelites were now encamped on the east side of the Jordan just north of the Dead Sea, across the river from **Jericho**; they had reached the threshold of the Promised Land. They looked on the period they spent in the wilderness as one of considerable importance. They remembered it regularly in covenant renewal ceremonies (Joshua 24:6–10), and mentioned it frequently in their psalms, Psalms 105, 106.

Throughout the period of the wilderness wanderings, God had to put up with a people whose bodies were in the wilderness but whose hearts were back in Egypt. Although God finally led Israel into the Promised Land, He was not motivated to do so by any good He saw in Israel. God blessed Israel *despite* what He saw in the people. God's grace remains the key concept throughout the narrative—and all history!

Numbers 22–24 describes the efforts of Balak, king of Moab, to frustrate the success and advance of Israel.

Numbers 22

Balak sends for a Mesopotamian diviner, Balaam, son of Beor, who lives at Pethor on the Euphrates River. Balak wants Balaam to put a curse on the Israelites. Balaam consults God concerning whether or not he should accept the invitation. God says "No!"—and Balaam shares God's answer with Balak's representatives, who convey the response to Balak. Balak sends them back to Balaam, who again consults God—and this time is told, "Go! But do only what I tell you," vv. 1–21.

God then becomes angry because Balaam is on his way to Moab, and He sends an angel to confront him. The result is that the donkey on which Balaam is riding turns, leaves the road, and goes into a field. Balaam strikes the donkey to force it to get back on track. The donkey then pushes one of Balaam's legs against a wall—so Balaam strikes it again. When the donkey sees the angel of the Lord blocking its path, it lays down under Balaam—who strikes it a third time. The angel of the Lord then empowers the donkey to enter into conversation with Balaam. Finally, the angel reveals its presence to Balaam himself. The angel tells him that, although he may go to Balak, he is to speak only the words that the angel tells him to speak, vv. 31–35.

Numbers 23

The next day, after Balak takes him to Bamoth-baal, Balaam tells Balak to build seven altars and to prepare seven bulls and seven rams—which Balaam and Balak then offer up in sacrifice. When Balaam speaks with God privately, God tells him that he may not, under any circumstances, curse Israel.

Balak then takes Balaam to another location, the field of Zophim on the top of Pisgah, builds another seven altars, and sacrifices on them another seven bulls and seven rams. Balaam has another private conversation with God, and is told that he dare never curse that people whom God has declared to be blessed. Balak tells Balaam not to curse Israel, and not to bless them.

The ritual involving altars and sacrifices is carried out once again—on the top of Peor.

Numbers 24

Balaam again declares Israel to be blessed, and states that anyone who curses Israel will be cursed, and anyone who blesses Israel will be blessed. He adds that eventually a royal figure will rise up within Israel and conquer both Moab and Edom. Most likely the reference is to David, 2 Samuel 8:2,13,14; see also Genesis 49:10.

Numbers 25 and 31 deal with the Israelites' involvement with the Baal fertility cults.

Numbers 25

After the Israelites settle at Shittim on the eastern side of the Jordan River (to the east of Jericho), Israelite men have sexual relations with Moabite women. When these women invite the Israelites to sacrifice to their gods, they accept the invitation and involve themselves in the worship of Baal of Peor. (*In Numbers 31:16, Balaam—now a Midianite king—is blamed for this incident.*) The Lord then commands Moses to impale the leaders among the people. Moses commands the judges among the people to kill all those who have yoked themselves to Baal of Peor. A plague then breaks out which causes the death of 24,000 people.

After Phinehas, a son of Eleazar, kills an Israelite male and a Midianite woman having ritual sex together, the plague stops. The Lord then instructs Moses to declare that the descendants of Phinehas (a son of Aaron's son, Eleazar) are to be guaranteed a perpetual priesthood.

Numbers 31

The Lord commands Moses to destroy the Midianites. (The reason given for this military venture is that the Midianites are linked to the seduction of the Israelites referred to in 25:16–18.) The Israelites kill every Midianite male (including Balaam!), burn all their towns, take captive all Midianite women and children, and take all their possessions, cattle, and flocks as booty. When the Israelites return to Moses at the camp on the eastern side of the Jordan, Moses commands them to kill all the male boys and any woman who has had sex with a man. Only those young girls who have not had sex with a man are to be permitted to live. The Israelites who carry out this massacre are then to remain outside the camp for seven days to purify themselves.

1 The Old Testament makes frequent reference to the worship of the Baals (**figures**, *upper left and right*, **ILLUSTRATION 10C**). It refers to them as Baal and Anath, or Baal and Ashtoreth (plural: Baals and Ashtaroth). The nations surrounding Israel worshiped similar gods, but gave them different names—such as Isis and Osiris (Egypt), and Ishtar and Tammuz (Mesopotamia). People made molten or carved images of these gods, and sometimes fashioned them out of clay or terra cotta. These gods were personifications of the forces of nature, and their images had obvious sexual features. The beliefs and practices were:

- Although there is one supreme male deity and one supreme female deity, there are many local manifestations of this supreme pair.
- When rain falls to the earth, the male god (who lives in the sky and clouds) is inseminating the female goddess (who inhabits the surface of the earth).
- Rituals performed by people influence the gods. If people cease to perform these rituals, nature will grind to a halt. To persuade the gods to be sexually intimate, men have sexual relations with temple prostitutes to persuade the gods to indulge in a similar action.

The **approval sign over a crop** (*lower center*) points to the emphasis on fertility. The **symbols for covenant and law-codes crossed out** serve as reminders that these things were not the focus of attention in the fertility cults. Furthermore, because human existence was also precarious for numerous reasons, human fertility was an important concern. The issue at stake was not merely human survival, but human resources. Hence, the practice of the fertility cult rituals was seen as a way to ensure numerous offspring.

When the Israelites entered Canaan, they no longer had access to the irrigation system that the waters of the Nile made possible. Hence, they had to learn to farm Canaanite-style, and to understand what the Canaanites thought they had to do to ensure adequate rainfall at the right time.

2 Archaeological discoveries in Babylon and northern Syria have provided information about beliefs and practices in both regions. What follows summarizes beliefs revealed in a Babylonian writing known as *Enuma Elish*.

> *There was once a time when neither heaven nor earth existed, but only the watery chaos ruled by Apsu and his consort Tiamat.* (Apsu is the symbol of fresh water, and Tiamat the symbol of the primeval ocean or "deep." Tiamat is sometimes portrayed as a large serpent-like beast—the dragon of chaos or the dragon of the sea.) *Tiamat gave birth to various pairs of heavenly beings, but they made so much noise that Apsu and Tiamat made plans to kill them. Their plot was discovered by Ea, the wise earth god, who killed Apsu before he could put his plan into effect. However, Tiamat was still alive. She created a group of terrifying monsters over whom she placed Kingu, one of her own offspring. The stage was now set for battle. None of the other gods was able to stand up to the Tiamat/Kingu coalition. Then Marduk, a son of Ea, entered the fray against Tiamat. He was promised the supreme kingship of the gods if he emerged the victor—and he did. Kingu was defeated. Tiamat was split in two. Marduk used one half of Tiamat's body to make the sky, sun, moon, and stars. He used the other half to form the earth. Ea then mixed the blood of the slain Kingu with clay to create humans to serve the gods so that they would never again have to work. All the gods then declared Marduk to be their king. A shrine was built in Babylon ("the gate of the gods") for the worship of Marduk.*

A second group of texts from Ugarit in northern Syria focuses on the emergence of Baal as the leader of the gods. Baal is seen as the storm god, and the bringer of rain (and therefore fertility) to the land. Rivalry broke out among the gods—including Yamm (the sea) and Baal (the rain). Baal, with the help of his sister Anat (the goddess of war) and Astarte (the goddess of earth and fertility), defeated Yamm and his supporters—Tannin, the dragon of the sea, and Loran (or Lothan, Isaiah 27:1), a serpent with seven heads. The gods then built a magnificent house for Baal so that he could rest and concentrate on providing abundant rain for the earth. However, Mot (the god of death and the underworld) rose up against Baal and triumphed over him. Baal then disappeared into the underworld. Shaphash (the sun god) and Anat found Baal, brought him back to life, and restored him to his house.

Many within Israel and Judah practiced Baal worship—especially in the more fertile farming regions of the Northern Kingdom. Jeremiah insisted that the Southern Kingdom would fall because of its dabbling in Baal worship, Jeremiah 7:1–15; 11:13,17. The problem diminished greatly after the return from exile in Babylon in 538 B.C. As later units will point out, the Judaism that eventually emerged in the reforms of Ezra and Nehemiah was passionately monotheistic. Without doubt, some within Judaism refused to accept Jesus as the Son of God in that, for them, such a belief sounded too much like a return to polytheism.

10A The Jacob clan most likely settled in Egypt at a time when it was ruled by non-Egyptians known as the Hyksos. Several centuries later, their descendants were enslaved by a Pharaoh who knew nothing about the services Jacob's son, Joseph, had rendered to the Egyptians. The Egyptian rulers pressed the Israelites into labor gangs, and forced them to work in the fields and to make bricks and mortar for their building projects.

God raised up Moses, called him at Mt. Sinai, and used him in a series of events (confrontation with the Pharaoh, ten plagues) that eventually enabled Moses to lead the Israelites out of Egypt into the Sinai peninsula. Debate continues concerning the route of the wilderness wanderings. It is difficult to determine the precise location of the many place-names referred to in the narratives in Exodus, Numbers, and Deuteronomy.

The Israelites rebelled, murmured, and grumbled repeatedly during their 40-year journey.

- While Moses was meeting with God on Mt. Sinai, Aaron and the people made and worshiped a golden calf.
- The people complained about the lack of food and water.
- Some objected to Moses' role as sole leader, and to his being married to a Cushite woman.
- Questions were raised about the priestly authority conferred on Moses and his descendants.
- Ten of the spies sent to survey the Promised Land came back with a negative report about the possibility of conquering its inhabitants. A subsequent feeble attempt to conquer the land failed, and the wanderers were told that they would have to spend forty years in the wilderness.

10B Rulers of the Edomites, Moabites, Amorites, and other groups living to the east of the Jordan River did all they could to block the progress of the Israelites and waged war against them. When Balak, king of Moab, sought to have Balaam, a seer from Mesopotamia, curse Israel, Balaam eventually declared that he could not curse Israel; he could only bless it.

The Israelites managed to prevail over all their opponents, and eventually encamped on the East Bank of the Jordan River. However, while there, they participated in sexual rituals associated with the worship of the fertility god, Baal.

God persisted in patient grace, and eventually brought the Israelites to the East Bank of the Jordan River. To the west lay Jericho. The hopes and dreams of many years were about to be fulfilled.

10C In Egypt, where the Nile could be tapped for irrigation, the Israelites had access to a sure supply of water for both personal and pastoral needs. Because no such water supply system existed in the Promised Land, many within Israel sought rain for their crops and pastures through the practice of rituals associated with Baal worship. The goal was to ensure fertility of both soil and womb. Scholars suggest that prior to Judah being taken into exile in Babylon in 587 B.C., 90% of the Israelites worshiped the Baals 90% of the time.